THE
EFFECTIVE
LANDLORD

THE
EFFECTIVE
LANDLORD

How Owners and Property Managers Can

ATTRACT BETTER TENANTS, RAISE RENTS, and

BOOST THEIR BOTTOM LINE in Any Market

DAN LIEBERMAN

Published by Advantage, Charleston, South Carolina.
Member of Advantage Media Group.

ADVANTAGE is a registered trademark, and the Advantage colophon is a trademark of Advantage Media Group, Inc.

Printed in the United States of America.

ISBN: 978-1-59932-414-2
LCCN: 2016955032

Cover design by Megan Elger.

This publication is designed to provide accurate and authoritative information in regard to the subject matter covered. It is sold with the understanding that the publisher is not engaged in rendering legal, accounting, or other professional services. If legal advice or other expert assistance is required, the services of a competent professional person should be sought.

 Advantage Media Group is proud to be a part of the Tree Neutral® program. Tree Neutral offsets the number of trees consumed in the production and printing of this book by taking proactive steps such as planting trees in direct proportion to the number of trees used to print books. To learn more about Tree Neutral, please visit **www.treeneutral.com.**

Advantage Media Group is a publisher of business, self-improvement, and professional development books. We help entrepreneurs, business leaders, and professionals share their Stories, Passion, and Knowledge to help others Learn & Grow. Do you have a manuscript or book idea that you would like us to consider for publishing? Please visit **advantagefamily.com** or call **1.866.775.1696.**

TABLE OF CONTENTS

ABOUT THE AUTHOR

Dan Lieberman is an active real estate investor, writer, and consultant known for his innovative, streetwise approach to property management. Dan has spent the past three decades acquiring, renovating, repositioning, and managing rental properties from single family homes to large multifamily apartment buildings, for himself and for his clients and investors.

Dan has worked in both good and bad real estate markets—and in both good and bad neighborhoods. Like you, he has dealt with tenants who were delinquent on their rent, underperforming property managers, banks that shut down lines of credit, capital expenditures that exceeded original estimates, and vacancy issues that lingered longer than anticipated.

Through all this, Dan Lieberman has become a leading expert helping rental property owners increase their rental income while improving operations and reducing costs in any economic climate. As a property turn-around expert, Dan Lieberman has continually asked the question: How does one transform an average or underperforming property into a winner? Dan has seen how real estate has changed over the past three decades. What worked a few years ago may no longer working today.

Dan Lieberman is the former president of the California Apartment Association, that state's leading advocate for rental property owners and managers. In addition, Mr. Lieberman has authored numerous articles on rental property renovation, marketing, and management and speaks regularly at industry conferences and educational events.

Dan is president of Milestone Properties, a boutique firm specializing in renovating and increasing the value of apartment properties in the San Francisco East Bay. In The Effective Landlord, Dan Lieberman shows you the system for rental management that helped both him and his clients grow their portfolios and transform time-consuming problem properties into buildings that attract and retain the best residents.

Prior to renovating and repositioning rental properties, Mr. Lieberman received his degrees in architecture and environmental science. He is a licensed general building contractor. He also probably drinks too much coffee. For more information, visit him at AskDanLieberman.com.

TAKING YOUR BUSINESS TO A HIGHER LEVEL

Why do some businesses have lines around the block, while others next door sit nearly empty? Why do some buildings stay full with quality tenants even while others are experiencing vacancy and collection issues? How can a property be failing under one ownership or management but then become a great success under another?

These are questions I used to wrestle with as a longtime property manager and landlord, but I found proven ways to succeed. This book has the answers to help transform the way you do business.

For many years now, I've been helping owners of rental property turn ordinary or underperforming real estate assets into extraordinary ones. It is my goal to share with you my thirty-plus years of experience in this industry, as a renovator, property manager, and landlord. If you already own rental property, this book will help you move forward more astutely, productively, and successfully. If you are just starting out, this book will save you years of hard work and trial and error.

The Effective Landlord is a guide for real estate owners and managers who want to succeed in today's market. Renters today are savvy. They go online for advice. Their expectations and desires are influenced by watching home improvement shows on television. Even on the way to viewing your rental property, they are online, reading reviews about it.

Your tenants are your customers. You need to create an environment that recognizes their desires and adds value to their lives. That involves everything from the things you do to initially appeal to their emotions, to how you handle the move-in process, to what options you give them to personalize their space, to how you treat them throughout the tenancy. It doesn't necessarily mean much more work on your part, but by being unique and responsive, you will achieve higher rents, shorter vacancies, and ultimately, a much more valuable property.

Successful companies such as Starbucks and Disney embrace this philosophy. They are creating environments their customers want and getting premium prices for doing so. Yet most real estate books are written as if owners and tenants were enemies. This book shows you a different way of managing rental properties: a route to success by meeting your tenants' needs. In doing so, your rents will be higher, your life will be easier, and you will have more time and more money.

> 🏠 *In doing so, your rents will be higher, your life will be easier, and you will have more time and more money.*

A HIGHLY ATTRACTIVE INVESTMENT

The rental industry is booming right now for a confluence of reasons including relatively low interest rates, credit challenges for potential home buyers, demographics, and supply and demand imbalances. Consider the cost of financing. If you pay 6 percent interest on a million dollars, that translates to $60,000 in interest per year. If your loan is at 4 percent, that's $40,000—and that's quite a difference! You can buy a lot with that additional $20,000. The recent low interest rates created a much better cash flow from day one.

In addition, people need a place to live, and now it's harder for them to qualify. Prior to the financial crisis, you could practically buy a house if your breath could fog a mirror. Back then, tenants whom we were going to evict told us, "You don't need to evict us. We're buying a house." And that's just what they did. It was astounding. They couldn't pay their rent, but they could buy a house. Anyone, it seemed, could get a loan.

Not now. People who want to buy a home today are rediscovering that they need this thing called a down payment and that it helps to have a strong credit score. More people need to rent because they can't buy. Demographically, the baby boomer wave has pushed through our society like a pig through a python. We built thousands of schools as those kids reached school age. We shuttered hundreds of those schools as they moved on. Now we have the echo-boomer wave, and they've hit prime renting age. They're in their early twenties and coming. They need a place to live.

Meanwhile, there is still less supply than demand. For several years, not many rental units were built, because of the recession. That's been changing over the past few years. Developers have been jumping in and building rapidly, but it's still going to take time to make up for the years when little was done.

Right now, rents are rising, and values are going up. But it will not always be that way. You don't want to have to rely on the general market to determine your fate. You want to be able to add value and create cash flow so you don't have to sell when the markets turn. That's one of the beautiful features of rental real estate. If you focus on the things you can control, such as creating cash flow and long-term tenancies, it won't matter whether the value of your property goes up or down due to the market conditions at the time.

There is always opportunity, in both good times and bad, but we now have that rising tide that lifts all ships. You can make some mistakes right now and still do okay.

NOW THAT YOU'VE BOUGHT IT, YOU HAVE TO MANAGE IT

Most real estate books overlook the immense importance of good management once you have acquired a property. They dismiss this critical part of your investment strategy. Some merely suggest leaving the management to someone you hire, while you just focus on buying and selling.

A good deal on the purchase is important, but when it comes to rental property, how you manage your property has everything to do with maximizing your profits. Successful management adds tens of thousands of dollars to your bottom line over time. You must take seriously the need to add significant value by increasing the income stream and net operating income (NOI). That way, you can hold on to the property for as long as you like or until the best time to sell, instead of sitting on an empty property that you feel pressured to sell quickly, especially when the market goes bad.

My focus is on turning around a property to make a better profit for the owner, whether my partners and I are the owners or I act as a third-party property manager. I will be talking about the range of things that an owner can do to enhance the bottom line via sound operating tactics.

One of them is simply adopting the mind-set for success. You may need to change how you think about the landlord/tenant relationship. Landlords have to realize that tenants are smart and that the market knows value. Excellence in business, it has been said, is not what you think but what your customer thinks. In trying to figure out what upgrades to do or what services to offer, your market will tell you. You just need to really listen to your customers—that is, your tenants or prospective tenants—as sources of feedback and not feel you know everything.

People have become more sophisticated, and the business of landlording has changed dramatically in our technological world of Internet surfing and online shopping and comparison. Landlords need to be careful about their reputation. There now are review websites that talk about rental experiences, particularly where larger buildings are concerned. Expectations are high among tenants who have seen marvelous accommodations on HGTV and other television shows. Their desires might not quite match their budget, but they do want good value, and your job as a landlord is to give them good value.

The basics still work. The secret to increasing the value of your building may start with something as simple as using soap and water. If the place is clean, if it looks maintained, if it looks as if you care, that goes a long way. When I was still doing fee management at my former company, Horizon Management Group, we would evaluate ways we could affordably upgrade an apartment community. We'd say the three biggest bangs for your buck were landscape, painting, and signage. Such touches can go a long way and are a lot less expensive than a full renovation of each apartment.

I will go into detail about these matters and much more throughout this book.

DEVELOPING YOUR STRATEGY

Before you can focus on improving the emotional appeal of your property, you need to be clear about your answer to the question of whom you are trying to appeal to. Who is likely to be the typical tenant in your property, and whom do you envision as the ideal tenant? You must carefully consider such things before you can develop a workable plan for marketing the property.

You need to consider how your rentals compare to others that prospective tenants are considering. Your goal is to make your apartments unique so that prospects are forced to comparison shop on something besides price. If you can sell them on something special, they won't go elsewhere, because it simply won't be available there.

Your goal is to make your apartments unique so that prospects are forced to comparison shop on something besides price.

You also want to look for a "hole in the market." Let's say you're trying to upgrade your one-bedroom apartment. You learn that the community has numerous bread-and-butter one-bedroom apartments that rent for $750 to $900, and it has newer, luxury ones that rent for $1,100 or $1,200. That tells you there is a hole in the market between the $900 and the $1,100. You well might be able to get your apartment into that range easily and appeal to people who can't quite afford the luxury apartments but certainly can do better than the cheapest places.

Always remember that you are operating a business, and all decisions must be based on business strategy. Your business strategy must drive your capital strategy. If you are not careful, your building can become a money pit where the cash simply disappears. It will accept anything you throw into it, but doing that might not help you. So you have to think about each remodeling item that you are considering and how it will enhance the overall marketability and value of your unit. Not everything you do will add value.

Even on a tight budget, you can accomplish a lot if you use some ingenuity. It's true that you must always keep the budget in mind, but thinking long term is an essential part of that. You must consider wear and tear and future replacement and repair costs. And in the process of doing necessary repairs, you can also find ways to add appeal to your property so that you're not only keeping up with the maintenance but are taking your business to a higher level.

SAVE YEARS OF MISTAKES AND GAIN FROM MY EXPERIENCE

I fell into this field. I hadn't planned for it. I studied architectural design in college, and when I couldn't find a job in design after graduating, I started doing handyman work as a way to make ends meet. Pretty soon, I was doing work helping real estate agents get homes ready for sale. I then started buying, fixing, and flipping homes myself. Eventually, I moved into small rental properties and from there to larger ones. At one point, we had nearly fifty people on staff as we were renovating, managing, and maintaining multiple properties.

I viewed buying real estate as solving a problem. Why was the vacancy high in that property? What could we do to transform the feel of the asset when people first arrived? What additional items or services would the residents be willing to pay extra for? We would take over ownership or management of a property, do strategic improvements and changes in management and marketing, and in most cases, dramatically impact the income and value of the property.

In doing all this, I also made my own share of mistakes, some of them costly. And, along the way, I learned plenty about this business and what works and what does not. Now, with so many opportunities out there, I want to share what I have learned so you can add to your own knowledge and wealth, or if you are just starting out, get a jump-start on a lucrative career. Over the years, I have become increasingly involved in this industry. I have frequently spoken at conferences, have written numerous articles on upgrading and turning properties around, and have consulted with other companies and owners on how to increase their revenue and improve their operations.

At Horizon Management, I used to have monthly meetings at which everyone in the company would gather to overcome current challenges, work on best practices, and move our portfolio forward. I would use those meetings to teach how to stage rental units, how to deal with maintenance and reduce costs, and how to do the many things that I write about in this book. I share my knowledge of best practices and management and my enthusiasm for how those practices not only can dramatically improve your business but also improve neighborhoods and improve the lives of your tenants. These are the same techniques we use in our own portfolio and when I consult with clients.

Chapter by chapter, I will guide you step by step through the processes you need to consider, which portions of the property could be enhanced, and how to streamline your costs. This will add hundreds or thousands of dollars per year to your bottom line, depending on your property, and could, ultimately, add tens of thousands to millions of dollars to your net worth. It means you will be bringing in more money and reducing some expenses—and the value of most rental property is based on that NOI formula of income minus expenses.

You will get a collection of strategies and real-life examples for successfully repositioning your rental property. You will learn how to transform that property into one that people genuinely want to live in. And once you do that, you can dispense with all the selling and focus on creating long-term customer relationships. If what you provide stands out from the competition and gives the renter what they want, you won't have the collection problems and other problems most landlords have.

The benefits are clear: improved occupancy; less wear and tear on your units as you get better tenants, who tend to stay longer; and reduced turnover and vacancy costs. People will start referring other people to your building, which cuts down your marketing costs and downtime. You may soon have waiting lists. That means you can charge more, and all of that rolls into creating more value. Now let's get started!

CHAPTER 1

FOCUSING ON THE EXPERIENCE

*How This One Shift Will
Make All the Difference*

I have often seen a line of customers out the door of the local Starbucks while other coffee shops on the same street are nearly empty. Starbucks doesn't exactly serve an inexpensive cup of coffee, so it's something besides the desire to save a buck that drives all those customers to the counter for their lattes and espressos.

Nor is it the quality of the brew. Sure, the coffee is good at Starbucks, but what brings the customers through the door is the overall experience they expect.

Starbucks succeeded because it was able to go beyond selling coffee to sell an emotional experience. In the Starbucks environs, one indulges in coffeespeak. A rich vocabulary suggests a richness of flavors, and those cushy chairs and sofas invite conversational intimacy. The atmosphere itself adds value to the products and raises the prices.

Starbucks went to great effort to build and maintain a customer experience. It reproduces that experience in malls and on main streets far and wide. Seeing the effect on the bottom line, other businesses want to sell an experience as well as a product or a service. The customer, it seems, must never be bored. When business can also become show business, profits will rise.

What Starbucks offers is an experience. You can have your double caramel latte, your Frappuccino, your macchiato. It created a language and an ambiance to make the experience more enticing and reinforce a sense of community.

Disney is also a master at building an experience. The company realized that everything is show business. Even the janitors and maintenance crews are trained to treat people cordially and helpfully. When the customers truly feel like guests, they will spread the word. The experience has become the calling card.

THE THEATER OF PROPERTY MANAGEMENT

To build patronage, a company needs to create a series of memorable events. It needs to stage and script an experience that will engage customers in a personal way. It's a lesson that rental property owners must learn: you can add value to your property by scripting the experience for the tenant or the prospective tenant. It's important to think everything through.

First impressions are crucial. Your prospects will size up the building as they first drive up to it. They will begin to make a mental inventory of the pluses and minuses. They will be influenced by how you and your staff greet them. Don't forget the power of words. Think of what you have experienced when you call a doctor for an appointment. There's a big difference between hearing, "Sorry, the doctor can't see you till Friday," versus "You're in luck! We have an opening on Friday for you!" You must think about what you will say and how it comes across. Your words alone can add value—and that translates to higher rents.

The amenities that your apartments offer certainly will determine how much you can charge, but other influences play important roles too. There are a number of ways in which you enhance value, and they involve methods of leasing and marketing, services offered, upgrades, and unique programs and options.

It's all part of the theater of the rental property business. It's all part of putting some show business into your business. You're focusing on the whole customer experience. Everything the landlord does is the "show" and the tenants and prospective tenants are the audience. Whether they applaud or boo will depend on what they see, hear, and experience. And in your case, their applauding or booing can be measured in your financial results.

> 🏠 *Everything the landlord does is the "show" and the tenants and prospective tenants are the audience.*

Years ago, Holiday Inn studied the key points that influenced whether a guest considered a hotel stay to be a good or bad experience. The study found seven key points. Among them were how the guest felt when checking in, when first opening the door to the room, and when checking out. Even if everything else was not so great, the guests reported a great experience if they were happy with those seven key points.

There are, likewise, key moments when prospective tenants interact with the landlord that will make or break their experience. If you do this right, you will rent more quickly, keep tenants longer, and tenants will pay more. The difference is that your "guests" stay for many months or years, not for a day or a weekend as hotel guests do. That's a major challenge of running a rental property. When and how you communicate with your tenants makes a big difference. If the only time they ever hear from the owner is when they get a rent increase notification, that has one impact. If they hear from you regularly about matters benefiting them, that has another impact.

How clean is the garbage area? How clean is the laundry room? Those are the things that the resident sees over the long term. Tenants want to feel their building is well maintained. They want their friends and family to think they made a good choice. And that extends from their first impressions of curb appeal to the path to the leasing office and the many details around the property.

In one of my management company's first projects, we took over an apartment building that, frankly, was a mess. It had seventy-two units and twenty-eight of them were vacant—and it was little wonder. The units were in poor condition. The staff was scavenging parts from one unit to repair and rent another unit. There were inefficiencies everywhere. In addition, a year earlier, there had been a police chase and shooting near the property, and the building's poor reputation had been spreading.

We wanted to upgrade the entire property, but we had almost no money to do so. There were ten stairwells throughout the building. Instead of renovating them all, we decided to renovate one. It was all we could afford to do. No matter which apartment our prospects came to see, we made sure we took them up that one stairwell. The other nine had to stay ugly for a while until we stabilized and were able to do them. In many cases, this created quite a roundabout tour. However, it worked. Soon, we enhanced common areas and started renovating the individual apartments to a decent level, with fresh paint, new carpeting and vinyl, and updated light fixtures.

When we started re-renting, I made the decision not to raise the price. My client, the building's owner, was concerned. "Why are you spending all this money," he asked, "if we're not going to get any more rent?" But he soon saw the results. We attracted more qualified people. We attracted people who would not abuse the property. Yes, they were bargain hunters, but they were of a much higher quality than the existing tenants. We soon filled at least a third of the apartments with such people, and because they were getting a good deal, they were willing to overlook the property's reputation and put up with the people in the other two-thirds of the building.

Then we started working on improving the behavior of the remaining tenants. As conditions got better, many of them followed the good example of the new residents and ceased to be a problem. In the end, we only had to evict a few.

Once the building had changed its feel, we were then able to raise rents. When we did that, we lost some of those initial pioneers because all they wanted was a low rental payment. But others stayed, and new tenants were happy to pay the higher price. It all worked out great, but the whole process took about eighteen months.

Contrast this with another property. At a different building we took over, we renovated the property and immediately raised the rents. We spent $10,000 per unit to make them all like new. We attracted people because they fell in love with the place after the renovations, but within a few months, many asked to terminate their leases. They were not enthralled with what was going on in the neighborhood outside our community.

What that shows is that with time and patience, you can turn a troubled property around, but you need to carefully assess the conditions not just of the property but also of the neighborhood. If you can afford to make improvements and raise rents in steps, you often can get better results. Sometimes, though, you need to raise the rent simply because that's the only way to attract the kind of tenant you are looking for. If the rent is too low, some might not bother looking, assuming the living conditions are below their standard.

Though the approaches will vary, showmanship remains a crucial element. We gave people a vision of what these places would be like. That's what brought the money in that made it possible to do improvements. You need to get them in the door, and you need to create that upgraded feel. You build their expectations.

Yet, if the outside looks nice but the inside is tired, you're not going to get them and keep them. You need to deliver on expectations. You may not have the luxury of doing both the exteriors and interiors at the same time. We tried to balance our work on the outside of the property with our work on the inside. We always said that the outside brings them in and the inside keeps them.

You have to juggle the two. If you make the outside beautiful but the inside is rough, it's not going to help in renting. The best approach is to progressively do a little inside and a little outside so that you can attract and retain tenants.

At one building where we had that challenge, we put all the money on the inside. The only way we could sell people on those apartments was to emphasize, in our advertisements, "Don't judge a book by its cover." If they were willing to get past the entrance and come into the property, we were sure they would not regret it. We showed before and after pictures of the interiors and let them know that the ugly exterior was going to change soon. Of course, we had a rendering of that future exterior in our leasing office/ model apartment as well as a large "coming soon" sign in front of the property.

You have to sell the vision. You show your sincerity as you share the dream of what is to be. You're not trying to fool prospective tenants. Rather, you're telling them just what they're going to get, and you explain what you plan to do. The prospective tenants will view your rental offer as a bargain. In the case of the building I described above, we told people that the rents would be higher once all the work was done, but they could get in at the lower price if they rented immediately.

It all helped to make a difference. Again, you need to think through what prospective tenants experience when they first drive up to the property and interact with you. As the landlord, you must script that exchange. You must control the show and make it the best possible production within the budget that you have to work with.

ENHANCING THE SENSE OF VALUE

How do you create value? In essence, you make your product—in your case, your apartments—feel like something that people will want to pay more money to get. If your apartments are renting for $1,200 and people are willing to pay $3,000 to rent at the new condominiums in town, it's a good idea to pay a visit to those condos and see what they are offering. What elements do they have that you could have too? What could you incorporate so that your rentals feel newer and more luxurious? Some things will be easy, and others will not. And you well may notice, as I have, that the owners may be charging a lot for things that look horrible. A good observation combined with discriminating taste will invariably spark plenty of ideas.

Then you take those ideas and apply them to basic design principles. For example, you can create the illusion of spaciousness. That can be done with color and light or with mirrors. If you're doing renovations, it might mean opening up a wall. If you have two rooms that have a half wall between them, you still feel you have two rooms, but somehow, they visually borrow space from each other so the place feels bigger. Light makes a big difference.

Really, what you are looking for is quality. In the more expensive places, what are the quality things that you can adopt, even if just a touch of them? You might install, for example, a tile entryway into what is mostly a carpeted living area. In the first couple of feet you place the better-quality material. At the entryway, you might install an expensive light fixture or do a special treatment for the front door to make the place feel homier or more substantial. Remember that first impressions matter.

To help prospective tenants visualize the apartment, you can stage certain areas. Prospects may need help in imagining what living there would feel like. The concept of the minimodel is the most affordable way to rent your units quickly. Larger apartment communities can afford to take an apartment out of service and fully furnish it as a model, but smaller operations often use the minimodel concept, in which a vacant unit is used as a temporary model. Essentially, the vacancy is staged to create points of focus and make the unit feel homey. You might place on the kitchen counter a cookbook, a bottle of wine, and glass canisters containing pasta and beans, for example, or place candles and a colorful shower curtain and towels in the bathroom. You can think of it as a "model in a box," as it easily can be taken down and moved to the next vacant unit.

Time and time again, when a manager is puzzled as to why a unit hasn't rented for weeks, we'll send someone to decorate it, and within days, it will be under lease. The decoration need not be elaborate. As long as it doesn't look like junk left by the previous tenant, it will make a big difference. You don't need to make it look like a furnished apartment. Don't bother with furniture. Sometimes, we'll place an artificial ficus tree in a corner or create a festive atmosphere with balloons. You can stage a vacant apartment with items that cost no more than $300, and those items can be used again and again in other units.

Little things like that help to get people in the right mood to rent. You want them to feel comfortable and at home. That's why it's a good idea to offer chocolate or cookies at the leasing office. It's the kind of feel-good atmosphere in which people might decide, "Yeah, maybe we should just rent here."

There's a lot of psychology involved. Wise landlords understand the human mind and what drives emotions, what motivates people–in other words, what makes their tenants tick. When a tenant leases an apartment, it is essentially a sensory experience. The look, the feel, the smells, even the taste of those cookies all make an impression on your prospects, and you need to appeal to their senses and their sensibilities.

THE OPTION OF CUSTOMIZING

Let's say you have an apartment that you are renting out for $895. The guy down the block has an apartment for $800, and down the street, another guy is asking $850. If your place is not substantially bigger or different, prospective tenants are going to say, "I'm going to pay the $800. Why would I pay a hundred dollars more for yours?"

Turning your place into one they can't get anywhere else is the key to gaining price elasticity. You can do that by offering customized features. When you tell tenants that they can choose the paint colors or light fixtures, they may feel that the flexibility you offer is worth paying a few extra dollars for.

🏠 *Turning your place into one they can't get anywhere else is the key to gaining price elasticity.*

In effect, what you are doing by offering those options is making prospective tenants compare apples to oranges. You're not the same as the competition, so they cannot simply make a monetary calculation and go with whoever is cheapest. You are showing them how you stand out, how you are unique, and that's what will help you to rent out your apartments more quickly.

The beauty of offering the option of customizing is that it not only brings more money to you, the landlord, but will make your tenants feel special. They will see the apartment as a statement about *them* and that they'll have a unique experience there, not just a cookie-cutter one.

That's how so many products are being marketed today. Shoes, for example, come in countless varieties. There are websites where people can customize jeans to fit their body type. Likewise, people appreciate the opportunity to make their apartment more personal. They feel better about it, they're happier to show it to their friends, they'll stay longer, and you can charge more. You have truly added value worth paying for. And your tenants are buying the very improvements that you want to make anyway so that demand for your apartments will grow, and you can charge even higher rents later on.

The cost of the customizing may take a certain number of months to recoup. If the tenant stays longer than that, the additional rental charge becomes pure profit. And tenants usually do stay longer in homes they have helped to customize. And, depending on the customizing upgrade, the unit will usually be worth more and will rent for more after the tenant leaves.

Years ago, I worked briefly at an architecture firm. My job was to make tract homes look different, even though they had identical external and internal structural features. A change to the front, however, could make one look like a colonial, another like a Tudor, another like a craftsman. The builders knew they could increase demand if every house didn't look the same. People want to be able to say, "That's *my* place!" and not what amounts to saying, "I live in the fifth unit down the hall."

BUILDING YOUR BRAND

By adding value to your apartments and identifying them as unique, the customization option contributes to building your brand and establishing what differentiates you in the community.

There are a lot of ways to differentiate your brand. You get a different feel when you go into the Ritz Carlton, let's say, than a Motel 6, although you can do very well with either because each has its place in the market.

There are simple things you can do to advance your brand, but many landlords, particularly smaller ones, still aren't doing them. You can focus on services. You can focus on relationships. You can make things—such as the move-in process, setting up online payments, or maintenance requests—easy. This is all about your image. It's about how you wish to be seen in the community. It's how you come across and what people say when they talk about you. That's all part of your brand.

It comes back to creating the experience for the customer. You need to direct the show. And how do you figure out just what you should be doing as the director? Try this: Ask yourself what you would do differently if you were to charge admission to the performance.

Here's what I would do if I were to charge admission to view my apartments: In my leasing office, I would offer cookies and cold water. I would make sure the apartments were ready and spotless. I would script my presentation carefully for maximum effect. Anything I could do to make people feel good about my rental and their experience with me would help considerably when it came time to say, "Just sign here, and that will be $1,495." The best landlords do these things, by instinct perhaps, but usually consciously.

BE AT THE FOREFRONT OF TRENDS

Expectations have risen dramatically. We in the multifamily industry can take a cue from what the hotel industry is doing. Large firms spend hundreds of thousands of dollars or more on figuring out what people want. What colors are in? What styles are gaining in popularity?

You want to do what you can to help make your place feel modern and vibrant. In other words, it's out with the green shag carpet and in with the granite countertops—but within reason. You have budget constraints, so focus on affordable changes that add character. In one building, we replaced flush doors from the

1970s with six-panel doors that Home Depot sells. The difference in the look was dramatic. A wider casing around the door also can make a big difference.

You're after the image, and you can buy products that give you that image without the expense. Look at what hotels do, look at new construction, look at displays in home improvement stores, and look at before-and-after pictures in magazines. All these things will spark ideas. You don't necessarily need to have a genuine granite countertop; there are imitation products that look handsome. There are laminates that look like granite. If you insist on granite, you can now buy it quite inexpensively as long as it is a standard countertop size. You may decide to spend more on the granite and keep older cabinets and just install new pulls on them. You can make a kitchen look attractive without spending several thousand dollars.

For example, you can easily transform the look of a kitchen with the backsplash between countertop and upper cabinets. Decorative tiles there, or a border, will make the whole kitchen feel classier and upgraded, even with the same laminate countertop and same cabinets.

If the shower has cheap white tiles, you could give it a custom look by replacing a few of them with accent tiles, even handmade ones. Just four or five of those will transform the look. Replacing a plain old bathroom mirror with a framed one doesn't cost much. You can even buy frames that glue onto the front of those old mirrors. For about $100, you can buy an attractive light fixture for the vanity bar to replace those old Hollywood lights.

Install a dimmer switch or replace a standard outlet with one that includes USB ports for charging electronic devices. Put one in the kitchen and one in the bedroom, and during a showing you can say, "Oh, we have this . . ." Prospective tenants will be impressed at how high-tech you are, and yet, one of those outlets costs only, perhaps, $20. Very inexpensive touches can make a big difference.

No one can give you a book that says, "Here's just what to do," because things are always changing. Trends change regularly, as do the products that cater to them. You have to keep adjusting. But even if you spend $1,500 on those changes, you eventually will recoup those costs even if you get only an additional $50 or $75 a month on the rental. It might take you two or three years to recoup your expense, but the value of your property increases immediately. I often use the three-year rule. If the expense can pay itself back in three years or less, it makes sense to do.

It's not on a whim that the hotel and motel industry and the homebuilding industry spend a fortune on market research. You can tap into that research by looking at what the hotels are doing, particularly in common areas, or by visiting model homes to see what buyers of new houses are expecting. Then you can be the first to offer those features in your apartment. I especially like looking at new condos, as they share such commonality with apartments. So take a tour.

YOU'RE SELLING THE DREAM

All of us want to have the nicest home we can for the money we spend. Most people want to be able to invite their friends or family over and be proud of where they live. Even though they're paying rent for a unit, they want to feel it's a home. Even more than that: As a landlord, you're selling a lifestyle. The more you can make your apartments feel that way, the happier your tenants will be and the fewer vacancies you will have.

Consider the role of the services you provide and how well you provide them. Are you helping your tenants to feel comfortable and content? You may have a physically nice place that wows them when they walk in and you win them over, but how is your maintenance service? How easy is it to get something done, and what is the quality of that work? That becomes part of how comfortable your tenants feel.

How they communicate with you also influences their comfort level. Is it easy to reach you? How easy is it to pay rent, request maintenance, or ask questions about anything?

If you don't do those things right, their dreams will fizzle. They might have a customized rental that feels good to them, but those other aspects of your apartment services will either help to keep them or send them away. If your services are swift and dependable, your tenants will want to stay even if the apartment doesn't have what your competition offers.

In chapter 5 I will get into far more detail about issues of management and how to treat tenants reasonably to enhance the profitability of your business. You have to treat people well. It is all part of the experience. It's part of the Starbucks story and the Disney story. You have to sell people on believing in you. They have to have confidence in you, and they have to feel good about themselves. When you can do that for them, you're selling more than just a room or two and a place to crash at night.

As a property manager, I created a program consisting of twelve key steps, which was similar to the Holiday Inn's seven points that I mentioned. Years ago, we created a move-in and resident retention procedure. The first step was a congratulatory move-in letter, and the second was an orientation program.

When you're planning a vacation, a good agent sends you fancy brochures and, in many cases, a list of things to remember to bring (or not bring). It sets the tone for joyful days to come. There's a lesson there for landlords. Why not make the rental experience a little nicer by sending a letter and information packet to new tenants? The letter can explain what the apartment community offers and offer recommendations on restaurants, nearby dry cleaners, and a host of other services.

After the orientation and lease signing, we focused on creating a great move-in experience. We had a little gift in the unit after we gave the tenants their keys. We'd have a couple of bottles of water in the refrigerator and a warm welcome note to set the tone. With such thoughtfulness, the tenant feels the glass is half full, not half empty, if a problem arises later on.

Throughout the tenancy, we checked in with the resident multiple times: after forty-eight hours, one week, four months, etc. After tenants move in, you want to check in within two days to make sure everything is okay. You check in a week later because they usually have different questions then. A few months prior to the lease running out we would check in to see if they had any maintenance needs or any other issue that we needed to address. The schedule was scripted to help keep people longer.

Most landlords tend to deal with the 10 or 15 percent of tenants who are a big problem and with the 10 or 15 percent they love. They feel surprised when they get a move-out notice from someone in the 70 percent they ignore. When businesses lose customers, it's mostly due to neglect. The question that landlords should be asking is: "How do we keep the majority who are good people without having to spend too much time doing it?"

The people in the middle, the people who don't cause a fuss and who pay their rent regularly, want to feel special too. When you move to a new place, it's a stressful time, by definition. There's a lot going on in your life. You have to make arrangements, hire moving vans, change utilities, and deal with all sorts of things—maybe a new job at the same time. That's the time when you need to feel pampered a bit. But as most people who have lived in apartments know, that just doesn't happen. If you are the landlord who does make it happen, word will get around. You start getting referrals from contented tenants who tell their friends. Soon, nobody wants to leave, because their friends live there, their kids' friends live there, and they walk their dogs together. You are building stability.

Vacancy and turnover lead to the biggest costs in rental housing. Cutting that down by even 20 percent is significant. One study found that over 60 percent of turnover in apartments was totally controllable. For the most part, people don't move for reasons such as they're leaving town or have lost their job. They move because they are fed up with poor maintenance or they feel ignored when they try to call the manager or building owner, and as a result, they come to perceive their rent as too high for what they get in return.

Sometimes you need to bring in a fresh set of eyes to look at your challenges. We operated one building where it was hard to find the leasing office if you hadn't been there before. None of us had realized that. After all, we knew where to go. But when we brought in someone to assess the experience of a newcomer, we learned that visitors often felt frustrated by the length of time it took to figure out where the office was. With just a few signs, the problem went away.

It's all about setting that mood, creating that experience. If people are already frustrated by the time they see the apartment, even if they love it, they probably won't rent it. And if you reduce the rent to make up for your lapses, you are throwing money away.

You can cut your turnover in half simply by keeping people happier—within reason, of course. A small percentage of tenants will complain about everything, no matter how well you perform as a landlord. In general, though, people just want to feel special and they want something unique. That's what will make them stay. And if you don't have vacancy and turnover, life is easier, you have more money in your pocket, and you have the dream.

CHAPTER 2

CREATING A NEW IMAGE
How to Transform Your Property

I imagined my buff body, toned from a daily swim in the lap pool, visible just beyond the glass block wall. It was years ago, and I was working in downtown San Francisco. That pool at a nearby health club seemed to be calling my name. I joined the gym because of it. I knew it was the place for me.

But here's the interesting thing. In all the time I spent at the gym, I used that pool just once. What sold me on the club wasn't the reality of how my time there would be spent. I joined because of the image I wanted for myself. I could see myself as a better person and envisioned good things.

The lesson there for landlords is inescapable.

You want your prospective tenants to know that you have just the place for them. You will find that a showing turns into a rental much more quickly when you can sell the prospect on an image of how life there will be. Whether you offer a high-end barbecue area or put up a handsome trellis over a brick walkway, you will do well if you can, in some way, help people imagine themselves enjoying life at your apartments. They may never use the barbecue, but it's the thought that counts.

THE THREE-MINUTE RULE

We emphasize the importance of curb appeal and first impressions and what we call the three-minute rule—that is, you basically have three minutes to make an emotional appeal to your prospective tenants. Otherwise, you'll lose them.

If you have a larger property, and you're walking with prospects along the tour path, you need to come up with some "wow" factor at least every three minutes if you hope to keep them. That means you need things to point out to them, whether flowers, fountains, classic gates, or as I once heard it explained, "areas of ambience." You want to create spots where people will think they'll want to spend time, even if they never do.

The goal is to create an impression of value. As you're focusing on your amenities, think about those "wow" factors and how they compare to what your prospects might find elsewhere. And remember that amenities include more than the physical facilities. The extent and quality of your services are also amenities that add value to your business. That's why Starbucks can charge so much for a cup of coffee.

🏠 *The goal is to create an impression of value.*

How do you enhance those first impressions? A good place to start is to focus on the common area. The nice thing about common area upgrades is they don't cost a lot on a per-unit basis. If you have a thirty-unit building and are willing to spend $2,000 per unit, you have $60,000 to enhance the feel and tenor of your building. That $2,000 per apartment isn't going to get you very far, however, if you spend all of it on the units. Just buying new flooring for each apartment would use up the whole budget. By focusing instead on the common areas, you can do much more to enhance the building's appeal while keeping to your budget.

Residents don't eat and sleep in the common areas, of course, so you also want to consider first impressions inside each unit. The same things that sell a home are what sell an apartment. Kitchens and baths are of utmost importance. Your improvements might be simple. As I mentioned, sometimes all you need is a bold paint color or a nice light fixture. You may decide, however, on a more thorough update. You may need to change the countertop and install new cabinets or cabinet fronts.

Don't be too quick to install new cabinets, however. A coat or two of paint can go a long way. We had buildings with quality wooden cabinets, but they were old and beaten up and dark. It made sense to just paint them, and once we did, the place looked bright and like new. We painted a wall yellow, and the kitchen felt warm and sunny and homey. Before, it had felt dark and institutional.

So it's good to focus on kitchens and baths, but you don't have to break the bank. The nice thing about paint is it's cheap and you can be bold, and if you change your mind, it's an easy fix as opposed to tile, which is going to be there for thirty years regardless. You might even give some tenants the option of painting their own apartments. We allow that, although we want to know when they're doing it so that we can instruct them on how to do it right. We don't want the paint ending up on the carpet. As I mentioned before, we have also found that apartments rent more easily if we give people the choice of a color for an accent wall. That too lets them customize.

ALONG THE "MARKETING CORRIDOR"

As part of the theater of salesmanship, you want to think about the experience that newcomers to your property will have, starting from the time they drive up. What is the first "wow" factor there? What will be their impression?

First things first: where will you meet, how will they find you, and where will you take them? If you have a place with a leasing office, you want to think about their path to the office and also the path you will take together from there to the apartment.

Your office may be delightful, but if your prospects have trouble finding it, they will feel frustrated by the time they get to the door. They will hardly be in a mood to rent. They have wasted their time meandering around the property, for lack of clear direction. This happens more often than you might imagine. The signs, if there are any, are in sad shape, and the parking lot is shabby. The first impression is dismal. The sale is lost before it can begin. You can avoid that by thinking through what a prospect is likely to experience and by making sure that signs are visible and clear.

Also, think about what the prospect will see along the path to the apartment if you get that far. It may not be a direct path, particularly in a larger complex. If you have amenities such as a pool or fitness center, you might wander by them on the way. Show off the nice features—the barbecue grills, the pet walk area—and avoid any areas you would rather not emphasize. *What you're selling is the future, not reminders of the past.* You can route your path around problem areas as long as your path doesn't feel too roundabout. If the work you intend to do is incomplete, you may need to sell the vision in other ways. You could show a rendering of what the property will look like when finished. If the complex has several buildings, you could paint one of them and explain that the others will look like that within a year.

"THE MARKETING CORRIDOR"

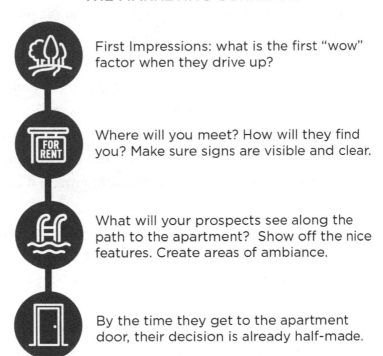

First Impressions: what is the first "wow" factor when they drive up?

Where will you meet? How will they find you? Make sure signs are visible and clear.

What will your prospects see along the path to the apartment? Show off the nice features. Create areas of ambiance.

By the time they get to the apartment door, their decision is already half-made.

We call this pathway the marketing corridor, and it's your chance to sell prospective tenants on the community and what it has to offer, even before you arrive at the apartment and sell them on its features. All along the corridor, the tour is scripted: what you say, where you go, even whom you talk to. The maintenance guy, for example, might appear to pick something off the floor just to show your staff is on top of things. You have to think about what will happen and what could happen. You have to rehearse your "script" and inspect the path before the tenant shows up, or you could face some sorry surprises, as in, "Oh no! Someone vomited on the path last night!"

You want to get to the site early, go into the apartment, and turn the lights on. When the prospects walk into the apartment, it should feel good to them. You could have soft music playing. You should adjust the heat or air conditioning so the apartment is comfortable. You might open a window to freshen the air.

Avoid any chance that your prospects might meet a problem tenant who might choose that moment to register a complaint with you. Ideally, as you're walking by, happy tenants will greet you and thank you for your service. You don't want some angry tenant to come up to you and say, "Hey, what's this about my rent increase I got last night?"

If you're doing everything right, that kind of nightmare is less likely. If tenants are pleased, overall, they will be predisposed to greet the newcomer with a positive comment, such as "Hey, this is a good place." You can script that too if you feel the need.

I always think a modeled apartment is better than a vacant one for showings. We recently had two vacancies, and we hadn't had the time to get them ready. So I told the manager, "I want you to find someone else who has the same floor plan and keeps an attractive apartment. And here's what we'll do. We'll offer them $100 for the use of their apartment, as a model, and we'll offer them $100 for every apartment we rent. Tell the prospective tenants that the apartment they would rent was just vacated and is a mess so you first want to show them what it will look like when it's ready." In our case, the manager took the prospects to the model apartment, and the residents there sang the praises of the place. It certainly didn't hurt that they were getting a bonus if we got a lease. We soon had both apartments rented.

For a very small investment, you get quite a return just by staging it that way. And the main reason it works is that someone besides you—someone who actually lives there—tells people how wonderful you are. That's always stronger than saying it yourself.

SIMPLE UPGRADES THAT GO FAR

As you create the new image for your apartments, you can add some relatively simple touches that will do much to enhance the atmosphere and, ultimately, the value of your property. I've already mentioned a number of things you can do, such as painting and landscaping. Let's take a look at some other upgrades that will add value to your property—and money to your bank account.

In the bathroom, for example, instead of having a vinyl floor, you could tile the entire floor and put up a shower curtain. The concept behind this is that bathrooms are relatively small and tile is a luxury item. You can get a lot of class and a lot of bang for your dollar without spending much because even though you're using an expensive product, you're likely only covering thirty square feet. In addition, you can avoid the expense of installing shower doors. For the same amount of money, you can have an impressive tile floor rather than a cheap vinyl one. That's one way to stretch your dollars to much better effect.

And you can add a few accent tiles in the bathroom. If you tile the entire shower surround, or the floor, in white, it will look bland. It's no more expensive to add a few colored tiles while you're having the work done. It's the same per-square-foot price for the installation, so you might as well add some interest from the start.

When you upgrade appliances, remember this concept: most of the cost is for the basic product, and what you pay for upgrades beyond that will give you much more for little cost. A basic stove, for example, may cost $279. For $50 more, you get the white-on-white appliance with a nice display. It doesn't cost much more to go to the upgraded appliance. It gives a wow factor. Most companies today are either buying standard appliances or going all the way up to stainless steel to make the apartment look like a condo. I've even seen stainless steel paint.

You could consider installing a set of glass doors in one of the kitchen cabinets. If you are spending $1,500 for new cabinets anyway, you can inexpensively add a couple of glass doors so that the tenants can display their nice china or other special items. The doors give the kitchen a classy look and cost, maybe, $10 more per door. Sometimes, we'll install the glass doors next to the dining area for a nice display area.

Instead of replacing old countertops, consider reglazing them. It can cost quite a bit to replace countertops, not just because of the expense of the material but also because you have to remove the sink and may need to replace it and all the plumbing that goes with it. All that involves material and labor as well. A basic laminate countertop project might cost $600 to $800, even if the product itself is only $200 to $300. An alternative treatment is a fake granite reglaze. There are numerous products to make countertops look brand new, and they might cost only $150, which is a small cost to fill a vacancy quickly, even if the countertop looks marred up after just one tenant has used it.

If you reglaze, we usually recommend a move-in gift of a nice cutting board. It protects your countertop, and you might now get two or three tenancies out of it rather than one. Tenants see it as a gift; you see it as protection.

On your property's exterior, take a close look at the entrance-way. That's where you set the tone whenever people drive up to the property. The feeling of a higher-end product is what you're trying to create. You can renovate the entranceway with landscaping, color, and new hardscape. Colored, stamped concrete is a great product. You don't need long stretches of it. A twenty-foot-wide section will get people's attention. If you're repaving your parking lot, put the concrete at the entrance and near the entryway to the leasing office for maximum effect.

Think of landscaping in the same way. The emphasis should be on about 10 percent of the grounds, at key points where improvement will matter most. You can leave visitors with the impression that your entire property has been groomed that way. Even if they recognize that's not the case, they still get the feeling. It's like a *front* on the set of an old Hollywood movie.

I've already mentioned how high-quality flooring in the entryway to an apartment makes a good impression. Let me add this: the leasing agent should always be the one to unlock the door. Never let the prospective tenant do it. If the lock is sticky, the tenant will wonder from the start what else could be wrong.

TRENDY VERSUS NEUTRAL

Landlords sometimes try to stay as neutral as possible in their decorating, reasoning that they should play to the broadest tastes among tenants. White walls don't offend people. Prospects who have looked at six apartments with white walls will not be offended if yours is white too, but they won't necessarily be inspired to rent, either.

Think about trends. The paint-color scheme makes a difference. You may turn a few people off, but you are likely to impress others who are in tune with the latest styles. You can try bright colors and two-tone schemes. You're not stuck with your decision.

What works this year may not work next year, and it's easy to repaint.

Kitchen cabinets are another example of where trends come into play. Unlike paint, they are expensive to buy and install. When that is the case, it's best to stay neutral. We tend to be neutral on appliances, for example, because black is in one year and out the next. With cabinets, natural wood tends to hold its appeal, particularly rich cherry and oak, which tend to be timeless. But if the finish does get to the point where it is out of style, then paint can be the solution.

In the 1980s everyone was into European-style cabinetry: the flush melamine front with the little wood trim at the bottom. Today it *looks* 1980s. If you go into any apartment that still has that style, you feel you are going back in time. Anyone renting that apartment is likely to get tired of it soon. By contrast, I've gone into buildings built in the 1920s, in which the cabinets still were attractive and usable. Someone back then invested in quality, while a lot of fifties-era cabinets simply have to be torn out.

🏠 *Whatever you can do to provide unique, quality touches that are in tune with the times will serve to get signatures on your leases and profit in the bank.*

If you're really trying to save money, a raised panel door works well, and it's paintable, so you can keep up with changing styles. Refinishing a wooden floor is another good way to attract tenants, though be careful about doing so on a second floor where you could create noise problems. Whatever you can do to provide unique, quality touches that are in tune with the times will serve to get signatures on your leases and profit in the bank.

SPACE, LIGHT, AND COLOR

Things that are bigger are often perceived as more valuable, and that's true for apartments. All else being equal, if I have an eight-hundred-square-foot apartment versus a six-hundred-square-foot apartment, I'm willing to pay more for the one that gives me more space. Generally, you can't add square footage to an apartment, but you can make it feel bigger to get higher rent.

When professional stagers help sell a house, one of the first things they do is remove clutter. That immediately makes the place feel bigger. You need to do the same when you are trying to lease a vacant apartment. Make it feel bigger. The clutter should be long gone, of course, but there are many other ways to make a space look bigger than it is.

One way is to change the walls, where possible. If you can reduce the wall between two small rooms into a half wall, the rooms will visually borrow space from each other and the apartment will seem bigger. Similarly, if you have a large room, building a half wall in it will preserve that spacious look but also divide the room for different functions.

Outside light also enhances the sense of space, as do any features that tend to open the apartment to the outdoors. A patio, for example, amounts to livable space in some seasons, and it brings in light, making the apartment seem bigger. In the prospect's mind, the patio space is added into the total square footage.

Mirrors can help, if placed strategically and tastefully. Also, light colors tend to make spaces feel bigger. And think about creative uses for the apartment's nooks and niches. A little area off the kitchen could become a home office; just put a desk there, and you get the feel of an additional room. Outdoors, a tiny yard can feel like a luxurious garden with the right plantings.

The idea is to make the most of every bit of space and create the impression that there's more space than there is.

CHAPTER 3

PRICING IT RIGHT

How to Determine the Proper Rent

If all your apartments are full, does that mean you're a great landlord? A real estate genius? A lot of times, people think that, because their building is full, they must be doing a great job. If you offered a $20 item for $15, people would line up to buy it. Does that mean you're doing a great job? No. It means you're probably underpricing your product. We like full buildings, but we want to make sure that the apartments also are renting at close to market value.

Basically, you're throwing money away if you're not charging enough. That's why you're renting your apartments out easily. Some landlords brag about how long their waiting list is, which tells me they're not asking for high enough rent. You need to keep a balance. This is a business you are running, and you must try to maximize the revenue.

Controlling expenses is important, but it's the revenue from the rent that really gives you your upside. Typically, your expenses might be 45 percent of your income. Let's say you trim a dollar in expenses and you gain a dollar in rental income. The dollar saved is only 45 percent of the dollar added. Your first priority, then, is to focus on income, and your second focus is to control expenses. The way to focus on income is to be sure you are getting *market rent*.

How do you get market rent? You get it by tending to the range of considerations that I have been emphasizing. Prepare your product. Think about the marketing corridor and the *experience*. Focus on the strengths of your property and maximize them. Make yourself special. The key is to add value and to get your prospective resident to see that value.

Sure, you're going to fill your vacancies if your rental fee is low. You're also going to attract tenants of a lesser quality than you would prefer. That adds to your problems, both with financial issues and turnover. It's a supply and demand matter. If you are hitting it on all cylinders—that is, if you create good advertisements, if your price is right for the type of residents you are seeking, if your product is attractive when they show up, if you have a good script and an attractive set—then you will have more choices.

If ten people come to see your apartments and five are excited about them, you get to choose the best of the five. If only one comes and you need to pay the mortgage, you might accept that tenant even if she's far from ideal. You shouldn't have to settle for the marginal. Your goal is to create such demand that you can insist on quality. That makes your life easier because those residents will stay longer, and they will treat your building with greater respect, so when they do leave, your turnover costs will be less. You need to keep your eyes on the long-term perspective.

DETERMINING THE RIGHT RENT

How, then, do you know where to set your rent so that you are charging what your property is worth, not more, not less?

It's a matter of knowing your neighborhood. You need a clear sense of what buyers want and whether you are able to supply it. Find out why people are moving to your area, and then define your competition and assess how you compare.

DETERMINE THE RIGHT RENT

 Find out why people are moving to your area.

 Define your competition.

 Assess how you compare. Look for rent gaps, potential opportunities.

It may be that you are in the running not because of that nice unit with the big closet. It may be just that you are in the best location. You're near public transit. You're near jobs. You're near an amenity that's desirable, such as the waterfront. So know your neighborhood. That might be what you're selling to prospective tenants, more than the specific amenities of your building. You want to see your building as your prospects see it. What value do people perceive? What deficits? You could have the nicest building in the ghetto, but it's not going to work for you.

Analyze your vacancies. Landlords so often think about averages. You may find, if you examine your rental history for the property, that 10 or 15 percent of your units seem to be the ones that turn over most, even though they have the exact same floor plan as the others. You want to analyze why those units are the ones that people leave. Once you know why, you can deal with those reasons. You may need to lower the rent for a time while you make improvements and add value to those units. By analyzing your vacancies, you can come up with a game plan.

There could be many reasons for a high turnover at an apartment that has the same floor plan as the other apartments: the view from the window could be of a trash receptacle instead of the wooded lot the other tenants enjoy, or it may be particularly dark in that corner at night. Some problems can be cured easily. We've taken over buildings where we noticed dark, isolated corners that invited drug deals. By adding light to the area and directing more traffic to those spots, we drove the problem away.

When you survey your prospects and ask where else they are looking or what they chose, you may find that you really have an inferior product, or you may find you actually have a better product but are just not presenting it right. You pay a visit to the competition and see that they're giving chocolate chip cookies to everyone who comes in and they're chatting them up. These are such simple things, yet you are losing people because you aren't doing them.

In determining your asking price, look at the brackets. If you want $1,000, maybe a price of $995 is going to get you more tenants. Otherwise, prospects may never see your property come up in a search. What is the range people are considering? Are they looking at apartments like yours, priced from $800 to $1,200? If you're at the high end, you want to make sure you're staying within the bracket. When you include your additional charges, you're getting $1,295, but your actual rent of $1,195 keeps you in the range. You get people in the door so that you have a chance to show them the value you offer. In this day and age of online searching, you must pay attention to those brackets.

This is all part of examining the experience of the person who is coming to see your apartment. Your prospects' journey to your apartment typically begins when they see an ad somewhere or they receive a referral from a friend. Then they call you, and if you have good phone skills and keep them in play, they will drive over to see you. On the way, they see the neighborhood and then your property. They see the front lawn and the flowers—or the lack of flowers. They pull in and see the parking lot. They notice what kind of cars are there. If beer bottles are lying around, they see those. They see the condition of the buildings.

They walk up to meet you at the leasing office, or at the appointed spot, and you try to make a good first impression. Well, you're way past the first impression. The first impression comes much earlier than we imagine. It comes right when the prospect first touches fingers to keyboard to search for apartments.

You don't really set the rents. Tenants do. Ultimately, it is the market that determines whether your rental fees are too high or too low. You can help create that demand, and the market will reflect whether you are successful: if the rent is too high, people will leave; if it's not too high, they will come and stay. Ultimately, tenants tell you. The market tells you what level your rent should be at. If landlords were the ones who set the rental rates, they would never have a cash flow problem. They would just set rental rates high enough to cover all their costs and pay for their vacation. People would magically come in and pay whatever was asked.

It takes experience in a particular neighborhood, or area, to determine just where to set the rent. It's a matter of trial and error.

Nobody is happy to part with money. People view the rent they pay on an apartment as a cost. Your job is to turn it from a cost into a value. Money is hard to come by for your residents. They're looking for a good return. Your job, as landlord, is to sell the value.

Some people invariably will object that your rates are too high, so be prepared for that. You may be at a price point they are not used to paying. Emphasize what is included in the rental rate. You will be highlighting the value, but remember, that value comes from a lot more than the physical product. It also comes from the services and from the location. So much depends on what you say and how you present yourself. You can preprint flyers that list "fifty reasons to move here." You can present testimonials from other residents. You can do many things to reinforce the positive perceptions. That's how you maximize your rental rate.

🏠 *People view the rent they pay on an apartment as a cost. Your job is to turn it from a cost into a value.*

PRICING BY POINTS

Not all the apartments in the same building go for the same rent, because some offer an extra bedroom or some other amenity. But you may find that one apartment is bringing in $200 more than a very similar one. How does that happen? Let's say you bought a sixty-unit building in which there were forty with two bedrooms and twenty with one bedroom, and you set the prices at $1,000 for two bedrooms and $800 for one bedroom. Over time, you would find that certain units were far more in demand than others.

There could be many reasons why that would be so, but you could learn a lot from talking with residents and prospects. I have had two-story buildings in which the first floor units were $100 more than the second floor units because tenants tended to be families that wanted the small yard and patio for the kids. The first-floor units were always in high demand. I've had other buildings in which the second-floor units were in higher demand because of the view. Each property is unique, and I think of each unit as being unique as well.

When I'm surveying a property, I give points to each aspect of each unit. Factors in my unit-by-unit inspection include:

- How good is the view from this unit?

- How good is the outdoor living space at this unit?

- What is the condition of the unit?

- How is the layout?

I assign points to each of these factors and dollar amounts to each point. A corner unit with windows on two sides, giving it a nicer feel, might be $25 more. One with a larger patio might also be $25 more. In a building of sixty units, you easily could end up with a dozen or more rental rates. The point system accounts for why certain units are in greater demand and evaluates them.

HOW TO RAISE RENT

You must know your market not only when setting the rent but also when raising it. You need a sense of pricing that is in line with the market. Whether the tenant will be willing to pay that higher rent, however, will have much to do with how good a job you have done, as the landlord, in the past year. A displeased tenant is less likely to renew.

If you have been doing a good job, the tenants will know your value. They know that you offer some things they can't get elsewhere. You can highlight that value with an incentive system. We assign points during inspections and for referrals, and the tenant can cash in those points for a gift upon renewal or whenever they hit the appropriate point level. Some examples might be:

- Clean balconies earn ten points.

- Referrals earn fifty points.

- At the one-hundred-point level, tenants get a prize.

- At the two-hundred-point level, they get another prize.

For a reason as simple as being close to achieving the next point level, a tenant who has earned eighty-seven of a hundred points may be willing to renew his contract and pay $25 more per month rather than move out.

If you're planning to do some work on the building, do the work before you raise the rent so that people can see the value. Think of the energy and focus that you put into the initial leasing presentation. You should consider this to be re-leasing. Ideally, you should meet with the tenants in person when raising rent. Think through your strategy. Do you want to ask for a little more than you expect and then be willing to lower it so that the tenants feel they got a deal? Or do you want to set a firm figure?

Offer choices, such as a yearlong lease or a month-to-month arrangement at a higher rate. Longer terms build stability. Because they know they will be held financially responsible, people are less likely to leave on a whim or if they feel frustrated. You also gain control over when your leases expire. You don't want your leases ending at Thanksgiving when you will be in a dead zone for new rentals all through the holidays.

People may not realize the costs they will face in moving. If you need to, lay that out for them. Relocating is not cheap. You have expenses and hassles. A $25 or a $50 rent increase is less than the cost of moving. Tenants may have to rent a truck and spend hours packing and hauling. You may need to point out that those expenses exceed the rental fee you are asking.

If you also remind tenants of the inflation rate, the rent increase can come across as just a matter of fairness. Give a clear explanation for the increase, such as "our water bill has gone up 8 percent, so the rent increase of 5 percent that we are asking is actually less than our increasing costs." The tenants are likely to reason that if they were to go somewhere else, they would just face the same kind of rent increases because every business needs to keep up with inflation and the cost of living.

We recently had a building that had been 100 percent full. We raised rents and, for the most part, the tenants accepted the increase. One tenant, however, gave us notice that she was leaving and rescinded that notice a week later. She had looked around at other apartments and decided she was getting a great value. That's not rare. Once the numbers sink in, people realize they're better off staying put.

Your tenants may have to be reminded of what they have. You need to communicate benefits to them in various ways. If they check out your competition, they will get blank stares when they ask, "What colors am I allowed to paint the apartment?" or "Do you have a rewards program?" or "How much will my bonus be?" When your tenants realize that what they have isn't offered every-where, they will come back to you.

It's the perception of value that will keep your prices in line with the market and give you an edge over the competition. People want to feel that they are getting quality for their dollar, and they want to feel they are getting unique accommodations. If you can find that balance, you can charge what you're worth. The price will be right.

Don't just send out a letter. You want to soften the blow by offering a choice. The letter could say, "It's your anniversary, so you get to choose one of the items on this list. Please check an item and return this list to us. Also, it's time to renew your lease, so let's discuss the new rent levels." That's a far better approach than just hitting the tenant with, "Your rent is going up 17 percent."

If you handle this right, the tenant can feel as if the rent renewal is cause for celebration. The amount you spend on anniversary gifts is nothing compared to the cost of turnover if the tenant leaves. If you're willing to spend the time to get a vacant unit ready, to place ads, to take calls at all hours of the night, to schedule tours to try to rent your apartment, why wouldn't you devote that energy to the existing tenant instead? It might seem like a cost at first, but if you focus on renewals and on keeping your tenants, you're going to be making a lot more money in the long run, not to mention all of the time and hassle you will save.

CHAPTER 4

GOOD BONES, GOOD BUY

How to Find a Property with Potential

The building once had been nice—back in the 1960s, that is, when it was built. By the time we came across it in 2002, the apartments known as the Washington Townhomes were run down. The place had been neglected for years.

The lot was oddly shaped. The townhome apartments were built around the perimeter of a central courtyard, and a driveway surrounded the whole property. What that presented to us was the challenge of introducing outsiders to the inner beauty—that is, the beauty that we might be able to develop there.

Tenants had been getting into those apartments through the front door, right where their cars pulled in to park. They had to work their way through the parked cars to get to the door. However, in the middle of the property was that big courtyard. Each apartment had a private back patio with a six-foot-high fence that, essentially, walled off the patio from this courtyard, which had about four exits to the driveway around the perimeter.

Tenants had their own private townhome. They could look out on the courtyard from the second floor. If they wanted to use it, however, they had to walk around to one of the big entrances off the driveway.

We decided that the courtyard, which was underutilized, was the best feature of the property. We changed the ugly, Swiss-chalet-style entrance to a grand, pedestrian-oriented entrance. We cut the parking lot there and put down stamped concrete so people could walk from the parking lot into the courtyard.

We put landscaping on both sides of that stamped concrete. Then we put a fountain in the middle of the courtyard so when you went through this entrance, you heard the water flowing and the fountain would be your first impression.

That fountain was next to what would became our leasing office and community room, which had, originally, been built as a child care center and was just a junk storage room when we got the building. We tore down all those fences and replaced them with low ones, four and a half feet tall, so people still had privacy, but when they stood up, they could see over the fences and into the courtyard. That way, neighbors could interact more easily if they chose to do so.

We took the old, aluminum, sliding glass doors to the back patio and replaced them with nice, wood, French doors. When prospects came to see the apartments, we took them through those doors, which had now become, essentially, the front doors to the apartment. Of course, on a day-to-day basis, people still could drive up to what used to be the front door to bring their groceries directly into the kitchen. We upgraded other things, but we didn't do much more to reorient the units aside from improving and highlighting the path to the courtyard entrance.

It made a big difference. We immediately increased the rent for new tenants. We renovated the unoccupied apartments and had a number of tenants willing to pay more to move into one of them.

BRINGING OUT THE POSSIBILITIES

That project demonstrates how you can use your creativity and ingenuity to bring out a building's possibilities, impress tenants, and gain a substantial increase in rent. You can rejuvenate a run-down or failing building so that you attract tenants who are willing to pay more, and you make owning the building profitable.

A building has to have good bones, structurally and aesthetically, to be truly a good buy.

A building has to have good bones, structurally and aesthetically, to be truly a good buy. That is, it must not only be worth its price, but you must also be able to make money on it. The numbers have to work. When we're looking at buildings, we try to identify some positive features:

- Are the apartments larger than average?

- Is it a great location?

- Are there other features that can be enhanced?

- What is the quality of the construction?

Some buildings were just slapped up during a boom. Make sure that the structure you're getting is in good shape. If maintenance has been deferred in any area, consider whether you would have updated that area anyway to enhance the property's marketability.

As you check out the property, look especially for any features or amenities that stand out and make the property really special or have the potential to do so. It's a case-by-case determination.

Ideally, by buying and improving a property, you're solving someone's problem. Once you own the building and take care of that issue, you could cash in. If you're looking to get a good buy, you'd rather have the cancer (problem) in the neighborhood than be next to the cancer in the neighborhood. There's not much you can do about someone else's cancer if they don't wish to deal with it.

You don't want to buy a property where you are buffeted by everything that's going on around you. An acquaintance recently told me he was thinking about getting into real estate by buying a four-plex. I told him that, in that case, he needed to buy it in a decent neighborhood. In a bad neighborhood, you cannot influence what is going on around you no matter what you do. You're going to always have problems. You might buy a property cheap, but you're going to have to sell it cheap. You're going to have headaches the entire time you own it. If you have a larger building of, say, eighty to a hundred units, you may be able to create an oasis away from the neighborhood, but not with a smaller property. It's a matter of what you can control and what you cannot.

HAVE AN A-B-C PLAN

After you purchase your building, you need to decide which steps to take and in which order. You need an A-B-C plan:

- What do you need to do right away?

- What's phase one?

- What's phase two?

- What's phase three?

An important early step is to create that marketing corridor I described earlier. Establish the key spots that your prospects will see on a tour, from the leasing office to the apartment. If you are working on much of the building, you can ignore those sections on the tour but start out by renovating one room, or one building if the property has several, and show it off as your prototype. That's your step A.

Then you need to hit the ground running and make it work. You will need to keep up with the required work on the rest of the property, juggling between exterior work and interior work. You have to improve curb appeal to the extent that you can get people in off the street, although you must proceed in a logical order: if you plan to replace the siding, for example, you might want to hold off on landscaping right next to the buildings.

Your A-B-C plan, in effect, should set up your stage front so that prospects can visualize to some degree what the property will look like. Then it must deliver on those promises. Each property is unique in what is required, and as you experiment, you will find out what works.

TWO LEVELS OF UPGRADE

One option, especially if you're looking at putting a lot of money into your building and you have multiple units, is to have two different levels with two different price points. You may find that the lower price is what drives people to rent with you.

You may find that, without spending a lot, you can rent your unit for $1,295, whereas to get, at most, a few hundred dollars a month more, you'd have to spend thousands. The work may not be worth it.

You may decide to offer some premium units that get a full upgrade. For example, years ago, we took over an eighteen-story high-rise in Oakland on the "iffy" side of the lake. It was a great building, and we wanted to associate it with the nicer side of the lake. It wasn't really lakeside; it was a few blocks away.

First, we renovated the top two floors to a much higher, "penthouse" level. We charged several hundred dollars more for units with views and an array of other amenities there. Meanwhile, on lower floors where the view wouldn't matter, we did a lower-level renovation to allow us to charge a rent more in keeping with what people would expect to pay in that neighborhood. In other words, we reserved the most extensive renovations for the most desirable units where the improvements would have the most effect on the rental rates.

It comes back to weighing your competition. There's only so much that the rental market will allow you to do that makes sense. You can raise your rent only so high before you get to the point where people who are willing to spend that kind of money will go to a different neighborhood or look for the newer, fancier accommodations.

RESEARCH RENTAL RATES

It's important to research the rental rates in the neighborhood and region. The earlier you do that, the better. Consider whether the rental rates that a building's tenants have been paying are low compared to what they would have to pay elsewhere for something similar and find out why that might be the case. If the rates are in line with others, should they be? For example, other landlords may be charging $800 for their one-bedroom apartments, but are these one-bedroom apartments considerably larger than average or, more important, larger than yours?

The previous owner may not have maximized the building's potential. It could be that the units just look old and tired but are in a great location where it seems everyone wants to live. In the community of Alameda, California, for example, many landlords have owned their buildings for a long time. They get good rental rates, but they're nothing compared to what people would be willing to pay to live in that area. We went into one building and, just by cleaning it up and appealing to the demographic, got a rent increase of $200 or more per unit from new tenants. They were willing to pay that to live there. It was a similar case in another building, two blocks from the waterfront and four blocks from the historic downtown area. It didn't take much to get people to pay a few hundred dollars more per month for the privilege of being there.

You might have a similar situation on your hands. Check into it. Is there a hole in the market that you could fill? Is there an upside that people would be willing to pay if you meet their needs? And this is particularly important to assess: are there features that are not being utilized at this property that will allow for that bump?

The nicer the neighborhood, the more potential for such an increase. In a building I have in the prime part of town, the rents recently went from $1,100 to $1,450 as new people came in. Nothing else changed. The people who live there are all young people earning $60,000 to $80,000 a year. The difference between paying $1,100 and paying $1,450 was not huge for them. I have another property where we've also raised rents. The typical tenants there earn $15 or $18 an hour. For them, it's a big difference even to go from $1,100 to $1,150 a month.

If you're looking at buying a property in a neighborhood with that kind of tenant profile, you don't have the ability to push rents no matter what you do, because people just can't afford it. Anyone who can afford it is not looking for an apartment in that neighborhood. That's an important consideration.

When you're assessing the property, you need to determine how valuable it could be to you. You need to look at the income stream and moneymaking potential. That's always got to be the goal. It can't just be, "Hey, that's a cute building. Let's make it cute for the neighborhood." You're running a business. You're looking at how you can make more money in the many ways I've mentioned.

It's easy to forget that. You might be a craftsman type, like me, who likes to make places beautiful. Or you might focus only on numbers and fail to realize that the numbers are driven by the actual things you do at the property. Remember that after you buy, you have to manage.

Yes, you really are looking for holes in the market and unmet needs that you can meet. If you recognize an unrealized potential, you have recognized a source of income if you approach it creatively. But you can't just go on your creative instincts alone. The numbers have to work, and your research on a property may lead you to conclude that they just never would.

THE À LA CARTE MENU

With an à la carte menu, the concept is that you pay for each individual item on the menu. Traditionally, you order a complete meal, and you can choose to order your dessert separately. With an à la carte menu, however, when you order a steak, you get just the steak; the vegetables count as separately charged items.

From the restaurant's perspective, what would have been a $20 meal has become a $30 meal. That's where it makes all its profit. Many businesses think that way. A men's store, for example, will sell you a suit, which is the big-ticket item. Then, if you buy a couple of shirts and a couple of ties, that boosts the profit.

When you have an apartment, you can only set a price based on what appeals to prospective tenants. If you're in a neighborhood where the price range is from $1,000 to $1,200, you might be able to rent your really nice apartment at $1,195 or $1,150. Then you can explain that residents can buy parking privileges for $75.

Or you tell people that you welcome pets, but you charge $50 a month extra for pets. They're not going to throw Fido away for $50. Of course, before allowing pets, you want to make sure that your apartment can withstand the wear and tear. It should be designed for that and not just for looks. Pets can do far more damage in some apartments than in others.

With such add-on items, you can build a package in which the tenants are spending $1,350 in a neighborhood that may have been capped at $1,200. The key, though, is to avoid leading them to feel they're being "nickeled and dimed." Instead, you want them to feel that you're providing extra value and services for them and that they have the choice whether to use them or not. The little things do add up. It's not that you're ripping off the tenants. They're happy.

In one apartment building, we reduced a maintenance room to about one-third of its former size because we didn't really need all that space. The room was just collecting piles of junk, which may have been the way the maintenance guy liked it, but it didn't serve any other purpose. We carved up most of the room into little storage units of three-by-four feet or four-by-five feet, and we rented them for $25 to $40 a month.

Basically, we did that because these are small apartments in a great location. But they really are small. It was a way for tenants to store their extra items. It took a few years to recoup the actual cost of building all these things. In terms of immediate value to the property, through added income, it made a big difference. And of course, it was an added service that pleased the tenants.

Those $25 and $40 storage rental charges add up when multiplied by many tenants and can truly make your property more valuable as they enhance the cash flow. Just $25 a month on ten units is $3,000 a year, or $9,000 for three years. That's a lot of money. All these extra items can add significantly to your income. I figure I can get at least 10 percent of my income from nonrent revenue.

For example, coin-operated laundry facilities can afford an easy source of income. You could buy the machines and get all the income or accept a fifty-fifty split with the laundry company, for example. That's one tactic that provides an immediate upside. If it's a big enough property, soda machines and vending machines by the pool are a big plus. Think about whatever needs your tenants might have and how you can fill them. Is there a way to charge for premium parking areas? What other fee income makes sense as a benefit to the residents? You might even work out a deal with the cable company so that your tenants can get a below-market price while you also get a percentage of it back so you both win.

🏠 *Think about whatever needs your tenants might have and how you can fill them.*

Remember that all of those incremental increases from alternative sources can significantly benefit your bottom line. You can easily double your profits without having to raise anybody's rent.

WHERE NO LANDLORD HAS GONE BEFORE

The fundamental question to ask yourself is this: which money-making features could I enhance that no landlord at this building has taken advantage of before me?

The bones have to be good in the building so that it has the potential to help you make a good living as a landlord. You want a building where you can develop income streams, not one that will bleed you with costs. The combination of that potential and the way you tap into it is what can make the difference between struggling and thriving.

Again, as you're looking at the good bones, you're also trying to determine what you can do that might be different from what others have done. You want to put the prospective tenant in that position of having to choose between apples and oranges when comparing you with the competition.

The best feature could be as simple as location. You are in a prime location that has been underutilized, and people will pay to live in that area, so you can upgrade the property to match what they're willing to pay.

Before you buy, you could ask tenants what they would like to see in the property. Your market is a great source of ideas. When we were doing the à la carte menu, we sent a survey out with a list of upgrades to apartments. We asked people what they would be willing to pay for and how much. That told us what would be a profitable upgrade. In fact, we use those upgrades to retain residents: "Stay here a year and sign on for another, and we'll give you a new ceiling fan"—or whatever the survey told us was a hot item. And don't forget that those enhanced features stay for the next tenant. By directly asking what your residents are willing to pay for, you gain valuable insight.

Consider, of course, what the competition offers in amenities and features and whether you can offer your own take on those attributes that will make your place unique. If your competitors all have an outdoor fire pit with picnic area, for example, how can you make yours nicer? Whatever it is, focus on making yours better. Your goal is to be special and to make your tenant feel special. They want to feel that they found a good buy.

Never forget: your goal is to enhance the lives of your tenants. By doing that, you're going to reap the rewards.

CHAPTER 5

KEEPING YOUR TENANTS CONTENT

Key Points of Focus That Will Yield
Results Well beyond Their Effort

A recent survey showed that the average turnover rate in rental housing was between 55 and 62 percent. If you are losing more than half of your people on an annual basis, it's hard to stay in business. It certainly makes your business less profitable.

I will go into detail on the high cost of turnover in chapter 7. It includes not just the vacancy cost, which is huge, but all the costs surrounding it, such as the cost of getting the apartment ready, the cost of staff time, and the cost of any concessions you make. The expense typically ends up being three times the monthly rent just to get the apartment filled again.

The lesson should be clear: keeping tenants is very important. How do you keep your tenants longer? The same way you attracted them to begin with. You found new tenants by standing out from everyone else, offering something unique that people can get from only you. Now, take that same approach as you convince your own tenants that they should stay.

SHOW RESPECT AND CARE

First and foremost—and this shouldn't be a big shock—treat your tenants with respect. Take care of your residents. You're running a business, and these people are your customers.

There are many ways in which you can show you care about them. One is a move-in gift. Give them a thank-you for becoming your customer. That gift can be anything from a small package of goodies, sitting on the kitchen counter when they move in, to something larger. It sets the tone.

Then, throughout their tenancy, you want to take care of them by following up on maintenance requests—being proactive, ideally—checking in with them and building communication. Residents shouldn't have to work at being your customers. It's very frustrating to call someone several times to fix the same problem. That dissatisfaction ultimately results into their moving out at the end of the lease, sometimes before. You have cost yourself a lot of money without realizing it by neglecting your tenants' needs.

An interesting survey showed that only 80 percent of maintenance repairs are completed properly, to the resident's satisfaction, the first time they're done. That means that one out of five times, after you send someone over to do a repair, the resident doesn't think it was done. And how the resident views it is what really matters.

It's a simple and good practice to do follow-up calls: "I just want to check if the maintenance was done and completed to your satisfaction." Tenants talk to one another, and making calls like that will help you to rise to a higher level of esteem in their eyes. You show you care. If you're particularly busy, you can shoot an e-mail off just to check: "Just wanted to make sure that maintenance showed up today when they said they would and that everything was taken care of." If you get a yes in response, you're done. That e-mail could certainly come in handy later in court if the tenant hasn't paid you for two months and claims the whole reason was that maintenance was never done. It's a good idea to have that earlier expression of satisfaction in writing. That's why it's good to keep a record of your e-mail exchanges.

As a reward to good tenants who sign on for a second year, you can give them a gift, another after year two, and one after year three. Or you could give them an upgrade to their apartment, which I prefer to do because the upgrade permanently improves the value of the apartment. But even an outright gift, such as a flat-screen television costing $300, is a lot less than the $3,000 you would pay in costs if you lost that tenant and had to get the apartment ready for the next one. The gift is cheap when you consider the benefit of a continued tenancy.

In short, the reason tenants move is not so much the price of the apartment or the rising rent. Often, it's the perception of neglected maintenance or slow or unresponsive management. Good customer service is essential. Respect and care will pay off.

🏠 *Good customer service is essential. Respect and care will pay off.*

No one likes a price increase, whether it's for utilities or for groceries. However, you can soften that blow by providing good value and emphasizing it. You might say something like this when you raise the rent: "Look, our own costs have increased, and we need to raise your rent to keep things going. It's going to be $50 more for the next year, but we value you; let us offer you this gift." If all has gone well, you have built a relationship in which the tenants know you respond to maintenance calls and take care of concerns and treat them fairly. They won't want to risk the big unknown of a different landlord. Keeping these four things in mind will help you to remember the big picture of what it takes to keep good tenants.

WHAT DO RENTERS WANT?

Above all, renters want you to respond to their needs. They want a sense of community where they live. They want to customize their home to personalize it. They want their rental unit to feel like a home.

If you think of an apartment merely as a commodity with nothing to differentiate it, then the rent is based on not much more than the square footage. It's easy to compare one such standard place with another in the community. More space, higher rent. The prospective tenant easily compares those apples to apples.

When a landlord adds "goods" to the product—that is, amenities—the apartment becomes more upscale and harder to compare to just any other apartment in town. "We have granite countertops," you can tell your prospects, or "We have dishwashers, and check out our large closets and luxurious light fixtures." You are taking the prospects to a higher level with your goods and also with your package of services.

Your real jump comes when you can sell the prospects an entire experience. Think again about what Starbucks did with coffee. That's what could be possible with rental communities. To do so, you need a thorough understanding of your market. It's a point worth repeating: you want to determine what your residents value. What do your current tenants like about the place? What could be improved? What would they be willing to pay for? Listen to what they tell you. It will help you not only target your market better in the future but meet the needs of your residents and therefore keep them longer.

THE MOMENTS OF TRUTH

Remember that you can help to ensure a good customer experience by establishing regular procedures and following them diligently. Following a to-do list can go far toward convincing your tenants that you care about them and that you are worth keeping as a landlord. I've addressed many of these matters already, but here they are as a punch list for success. These are some of the procedures that I have used:

O   After you have rented to new tenants, send a congratulatory move-in letter. Think of the package that a travel agent sends you before you go on a cruise, with pictures of where you will be going and what you will need to bring and a letter about all the exciting things to do. You can do something similar. Send your new tenants an info package and letter that basically says, "Congratulations. We're excited to have you. Here's a map of the community. Here's a list of the local utilities and other phone numbers you will need and other useful information." A package like that helps to set the tone of your relationship.

O   In that package, you also say, "Please call to schedule your orientation." You want to set up a time where you can walk them through everything that needs to be done. It can include signing the lease. It can include a tour of the apartment, which includes some self-help maintenance tips, such as where to find that little reset button on the garbage disposal. You can tell them about visitor parking, trash pickup procedures, and other basics. I recommend that you offer this orientation not on move-in day but on the day before, which likely will be less hectic.

O   Do what you can to give your tenants a great move-in experience. Reserve a parking space that is convenient for a moving truck. Have a move-in gift ready in the apartment when they show up. We also recommend leaving a small box or basket of essentials such as toilet paper, paper towels, and soap. If you operate a larger property and have a maintenance technician on staff, this is a good time to provide whatever help you wish to offer, such as hanging pictures.

O   Soon after they move in, you should again make personal contact. Within two days you want to check in with them and say, "Just wanted to see if you have any questions." You might get questions such as: Where do I dump these boxes? Where's the bank? Where's the nearest Chinese restaurant? Questions inevitably will arise. Ideally, you might check in with your new tenants after one day, but at our company, our requirement is for the property manager to check in with them no later than two days after the move-in.

O Keep a calendar, and contact them again ten days to two weeks later. Welcome them once again to the community and see if any issues or concerns have come up. Perhaps the hot water supply isn't satisfactory, or maybe they just need to know how to enroll a child in school. You will find that the nature of the questions is different from that of the questions they asked during the first few days.

O Send a survey and a follow-up letter. Offer them a gift if they return the survey, perhaps a $5 or $10 gift card to a local establishment. Basically, the survey asks, "How was your move-in experience?" and includes questions about what attracted the new tenants to your place, how they feel so far, and what they might need. The idea is to get a sense of what you are doing right and what you might be doing wrong.

O Check in with them about seventy-five days after move-in or two and a half months into it. This can be just a phone call to evaluate things again. Remember that all your attention shouldn't go to just a small percentage of your tenants, the ones who cause the problems. You want to attend to all your tenants and make sure their experience is leading them to renew their contract. Your relationship should go beyond just collecting a check once a month. If someone is off to a bad start by paying late, just a few months into the lease, this is the time to give a friendly reminder about the due date and to reinforce your procedures and policies. It's also a good time to find out whether your new tenants have any further concerns about their apartment. If they are happy, this is a good opportunity to ask whether they know anyone else who might be interested in moving into your apartments.

O   Give your tenants another questionnaire four months into the tenancy. The first one was geared toward the move-in. This one is more geared toward house maintenance and how they like things in general. Having lived awhile in the apartment, they will face a different set of issues.

O   About ninety days before their lease expires, we send tenants a maintenance survey and request-for-service postcard. This helps to uncover any undisclosed issues. If you need to attend to something, you will be able to take care of it well before expiration day, when you will let them know the rent will increase by $50 a month and ask whether they want to renew for another year.

O   As the end of the contract approaches, send a lease renewal letter explaining their options for renewal. State how much the rent will be if they choose to renew for a year. If you want to offer a month-to-month renewal, or a six-month contract, explain that those arrangements would involve higher rates and state what those rates would be. Tell your tenants about any incentives you are offering—for example, if they sign up for a year, they have a choice of painting a colored accent wall or getting their carpet shampooed. Your purpose is to outline the rental rate options and remind them of any rewards they get if they stay.

O   When tenants renew their lease, treat them as cordially and thoughtfully as you do those who are first moving in. Send a thank-you letter for their renewal, and let them know you appreciate having them in your community. Be sure to arrange for them to receive whatever gift or upgrade they have coming.

○ If a tenant chooses not to renew, follow up to find out the reasons. This is an important step. Through a follow-up questionnaire, you will learn much about what you might do to improve your retention rate.

You will notice that many of those steps focus on interaction. They aim to develop that all-important relationship with your tenants, and you should encourage them to interact with one another to build a sense of community. We have organized special events and parties and conducted contests and raffles. The goal is to make your residents feel at home. When you do that, you are well on your way to building a strong resident referral system, which is a key to effective marketing.

LOOK AT YOUR TRASH RECEPTACLE

When you conduct your surveys and talk regularly to your tenants, you will find out things that you need to know and that many landlords often neglect. These involve day-to-day matters that the resident sees and has to live with. For example, the lights don't work in the laundry room, or there always seems to be trash scattered around the trash receptacle area. Your tenants get tired of these things, eventually to the point of leaving. Your tenants are doing you a favor when they point these things out to you. It's your opportunity to take steps to ensure that your property is perceived as pleasant in more ways than just curb appeal.

The beginning of the tenancy sets the tone for the entire term. A landlord can mess up that relationship in many ways, causing residents to feel ignored. That's why you need to put some "deposits in the bank" at the outset—that is, deposits of respect and trust in your dealings with people who are, essentially, your customers. A landlord needs to develop a good track record because that way, when mistakes happen, as they inevitably do, tenants will be more likely to see them as aberrations and not business as usual at the property.

COURTEOUS, PROFESSIONAL STAFF

Take care to hire professional and courteous managers and staff. Ask yourself whether your property manager is inadvertently encouraging the tenants to leave. If you have a larger property and don't have as much direct contact with your tenants, you might think all is well and your staff is doing a great job. After all, the manager seems nice enough to you when you ask for something to be done around the property. But does that manager seem nice enough to the residents? They might be getting a very different response when they ask for service.

🏠 Take care to hire professional and courteous managers and staff.

You need to make sure that your staff understands the big picture. They need to really get their role. When you are hiring, look for people who are very customer oriented. They need to understand that the business needs to be profitable and needs to operate efficiently, but the way that happens is by taking care of your residents and your customers, within reason, so you don't go broke. You have to balance the resident needs and the profitability of the company, but you can make that a win-win.

IF YOU DO MAKE A MISTAKE . . .

No matter how much you do right as a landlord, one bad experience can taint your entire relationship with a tenant. To help deal with that, you could set up a "what we do if we screw up" response. Think about the steps that some airlines take to win back your good favor if your flight is canceled. Let's say the furnace malfunctions and the repairman can't get it back in order for four days. You would lend the tenant a space heater, of course, but beyond that you could set up a procedure. You could give the tenant a voucher for dinner at a restaurant, for example. That can help undo negative effects. If someone is inconvenienced for a few days, such a gesture will go a long way.

My policy is not to offer rent credits. That seems to be the first thing that people request: "Can I get $100 off my next rent payment because of this?" Once you open up that Pandora's box, the demands keep coming. Maybe you feel the rent credit is justified the first time the tenant asks. But don't be surprised if you soon hear something like this: "Hey, I'm not getting much pressure from the kitchen faucet, so I'd like $50 off for that." The tenants begin to treat maintenance issues as if you owe them contract concessions. At least a gift card to a restaurant comes across like an apology from the heart.

TENANTS WILL TALK

Don't underestimate the power of the Internet and social media. Tenants talk to one another. They can build your business to new heights or destroy your reputation. With most businesses, the Internet has become the new normal in how things work. People go on Yelp and see that your business has only two stars and not five stars, and they shy away.

I had that happen to me. I had a tenant who was becoming unreasonable and just wasn't a good fit. At one point, she asked, "Can I get out of my lease?" We agreed to let her go with thirty days' notice. She was supposed to get her deposit back within a certain amount of time, and I approved the refund, but something went wrong in the bookkeeping and she didn't get it on time. Instead of calling us to inquire what had happened, she went online instead and started a rant, claiming we had stolen her money. And that became the first thing that popped up regarding us when prospects did rental searches.

That's an example of why relationship is so important. We asked our other residents to do us a favor and write us a good review if they were happy with us. Soon we had a five-star review, then another, and it wasn't long before that woman's one-star review sank to the bottom. Among so many five-star reviews, a lone one-star review looks as if a lunatic wrote it.

Apartment rating sites will not remove these reviews no matter how untrue they are. They will only delete your phone number or your name or other specifics. They say it's up to you to sue people for defamation. And so a bad review stays online, no matter how malicious it is, unless you somehow prevail in court to have it removed—and who can afford the time or money for that?

I remember reading a restaurant review years ago, before the days of social media, in which the critic wrote, "Right after I sat at my table, a roach ran across it—and my dinner went downhill from there." The place was shuttered a week later. But these days, it's not just the professional critic who can hurt your business.

Anyone who has a beef against you for any reason could put you out of business.

Your best defense against any such affront is to build up a storehouse of good relationships. And the best way to build those relationships is to take the steps that will ensure that your building is full of contented tenants.

CHAPTER 6

ATTRACTING GOOD RESIDENTS

*How to Keep Bad Tenants
out of Your Property*

Finding and getting the right tenant is possibly the single most important thing you can do in managing your property. Good residents pay their rent on time, respect your rules, and take care of your property. Choosing the wrong resident can cost you money, drive out your good residents, and even ruin your property.

You already have an advantage over the average owner or manager because you now see the importance of creating the right experience to attract the most prospects at the best rent. Most people do not design their product and presentation to appeal to their target market. This is critical. You have to think about your customers every step of the way.

You've focused on creating the experience once prospects arrive. They want to rent. But how do you know who is good and who is not? Your goal is not just to fill your vacancy fast but to fill it with an ideal resident.

SET POLICIES AND STANDARDS IN ADVANCE

The time to figure out how you will determine whether someone is a good applicant or a bad applicant is before you start taking applications. Create written criteria for how you will evaluate prospects. These do not have to be published and distributed but will help you stay objective when reviewing rental applications. If nothing else, they will help protect you should you get a fair-housing claim.

Some of these criteria can be as simple as a rent-to-income ratio or minimum credit score. You can assign different point weights to different areas, such as stability of tenancy, length of time at current job, liquidity, and so on. Residents who tend to live at their rentals for several years, have a stable job, and have lots of cash in the bank are less likely to get into trouble than tenants with a thin rental history, a new job, and barely enough money for the security deposit, even if both have similar credit scores.

You can also set certain criteria, such as not accepting an applicant if you cannot obtain a positive reference from a previous landlord. Of course, the best way to show you have policies and standards is to make them visible. Having written criteria tends to scare away some scammers who know they won't qualify. You can allow for credit blemishes; few people have perfect credit. Certainly, if your property is in a lower-income area, your standards need to be different from those for rentals in the best part of town.

🏠 *The best way to show you have policies and standards is to make them visible.*

Always run an unlawful detainer check (preferably one that shows all filings and not just completed evictions), and it may make sense to run a criminal background check as a standard practice as well. Remember, the cheapest credit report is not the best. Spend a little extra, and get the information you need. Saving $10 at this point is being penny wise and pound foolish.

ATTRACT HIGH-QUALITY RESIDENTS FAST

Years ago, I assumed management of a building where the owner had been having a hard time renting the apartments. The vacancy rate was higher than it should have been, even though the rents were very reasonable and the apartments showed well. The owner didn't know why.

It turned out the reason they were not renting was that the place was never open. The owner did not live near the property, and the manager just didn't go to the office that much. She had the phone forwarding messages to her apartment. She answered calls, took care of things, made rental appointments, and met prospects, but she missed out on the drive-by and walk-in prospects. They were not renting, because the place looked closed.

It was not what you would call effective marketing. While some problems are simple, like this one, often you don't know what's going on until you dig a little deeper. The simplest factor could totally change your results.

Once, most people looked in the newspaper when they wanted to rent an apartment. Nowadays, most people search for apartments either by going online or by walking or driving around a community where they want to live. Translated into a marketing strategy, that means your best ways, today, to attract potential tenants are to maintain an Internet presence and have good signage and curb appeal.

Do not become completely reliant on the Internet, because although it's a great tool, it's just one leg that supports your marketing table. Think of each marketing venue as a leg on a table. These might be resident referrals, posting flyers, connecting with local businesses, etc. Then, if something goes wrong with one leg, you're hurt but okay. If you only have one leg and something goes wrong, the table collapses. Yes, your primary venue can be Internet related. It can be a combination of free sites such as Craigslist and paid sites such as Rent.com, Zillow, or a variety of others.

THE MARKETING TABLE

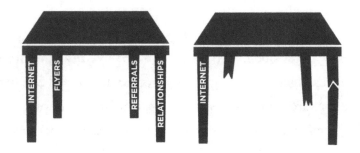

But you also want to look elsewhere. Marketing is an area where many owners are penny wise and pound foolish. Every day your rental sits vacant, it is costing you money. Within a few days of vacancy, you will have spent whatever that ad or sign might have cost you. By first determining your likely target market and then creating "wow" factors in your property that differentiate your rental from the many others, you will have a great head start over the other owners of property in your area.

In addition to posting ads on Craigslist and other similar sites, there are many things you can do to attract prospects to your rental. Sometimes, a small community weekly newspaper will get you a tenant that your online ads don't. Putting up flyers can be highly effective. You never know where people are looking. No matter where you advertise, pictures have become very important. People expect visuals. Your place needs to look good.

Get help from neighbors and local businesses. We have posted flyers at local businesses including hair salons, coffee shops, and dry cleaning establishments, among others. You can also make an agreement to buy a gift certificate from merchants referring prospects who become your contracted tenants.

But even when most people use the Internet as their starting point in their apartment search, the power of good signage and curb appeal cannot be overstated. These are your silent salespeople. You'd be amazed at how many people walk or drive by your property every day. If the appearance of the exterior makes people want to live there and there is a "For Rent" sign on the property, you will get calls.

ADVERTISING IN THE INTERNET AGE

In the days when people scanned newspaper ads for apartments, your competition tended to be other rentals in your same price range. If people wanted a two-bedroom apartment for $1,200, they would jot down places that were close to that "2BD" designation. And those would be the places they would call for a look.

The Internet has redefined both how people shop for apartments and the nature of the competition. You can post long ads with many photographs and video online, without paying a cent, and your prospects can find you through a variety of search criteria. So far, so good, but they also can find other landlords' offerings easily, and not just the ones up the street from you. They can easily compare amenities and related costs. That means your competition may no longer just be the apartments in your price range and right in your neighborhood. The Internet has broadened the scope of your competition.

Those considerations will influence how you design an ad for people searching online. You will want lots of pictures, of course. And you should be looking at the ads and websites of your potential competitors. If any seem to have apartments a little nicer than yours, examine what they offer and then move toward offering at least those same things.

It comes back to a familiar theme: What can you offer that might be different? How can you make yourself stand out? When you come up with something, mention it prominently in the headline for your ad—"The largest closets in town!"—or whatever you wish to highlight for your potential client base.

Amid the onslaught of online competition, it becomes increasingly essential to differentiate yourself. In the old days, when you were doing research, you might consult several books and research several areas of concern, trying to dig up information. Now, you do a Google search and, in an instant, you come up with 1,000,272 choices of pages you could read. How do you go through all that? People who are looking for apartments face the same sort of information overload.

Positioning yourself as special, therefore, becomes even more crucial in the Internet age. You need to be visible to people doing online searches, and you need to develop an attractive and useful website. Place the name of your website prominently in your ads and brochures, on your business cards, or wherever people are likely to see it. That will drive traffic to your website. Once they visit your site, they should be able to look at pictures of your apartments. If they are interested, they can contact you, and of course, your website should make that easy for them to do. If they are half sold by what they have seen online, your showings should be more productive. You will have fewer people wasting your time.

Your website should go beyond showing pictures of your available apartments. It should clearly establish why you are different. You can sell your amenities and service offerings, your resident retention program, and other incentives and deals. You could include testimonials from happy tenants pleased about the accommodations, the setting, and the management. Let others sing your praises; it's more believable than singing them yourself. Use your website to develop your brand.

DEVELOP A REFERRAL NETWORK

The power of the Internet is particularly useful in developing a referral network. I've long advocated resident referrals for many reasons. We had a reputation for turning around problem buildings. Some were in marginal areas and looked run-down at first. If you can get residents to tell others that they know firsthand that your apartments actually are a good place to live, you go a long way toward overcoming issues that dissuade prospects from signing leases. The referrals tend to presell them. The prospect may even have visited the apartment of whoever gave the referral.

We offer incentives in exchange for referrals. Back when a newspaper ad would cost us $150 or $200, paying people that much for referrals made particularly good sense. It is still an effective strategy. When a good tenant persuades a friend to sign a lease, that friend tends to also become a good tenant. You can significantly improve the quality of your community that way.

We have created resident referral reward programs in which we offer incentives to our current residents to refer a friend or colleague. This can be in the form of a cash reward, a purchase or gift card, or an upgrade to the referring resident's apartment. Sometimes, we've also offered a slight break on the new resident's rent for the first month to help entice that new resident.

A referral from a good tenant often is a double blessing. Once a resident has brought in some friends to live nearby, that resident is likely to stay put. Leaving would mean saying good-bye to those friends. When residents feel a sense of community—when they do things together and develop bonds of friendship—they are far more inclined to sign renewal after renewal.

E-MAIL BLASTS

If, for some reason, we're having a spike in vacancy, that's when we'll do our resident referral promotion. These days it is easy to collect the e-mail addresses of former and current residents. Even though people tend to change physical addresses, they tend not to change their e-mail addresses that often. An e-mail blast is an effective way to get out the word.

You can send the blast to existing residents and/or former residents. Basically, it says, "We have two three-bedroom apartments and a townhome coming up next month. We hope you know someone who would like to experience how great it is to live with us. We value our residents and want more tenants just like you. That's why we will pay you $200 if someone you refer to us before the tenth of next month rents an apartment." It costs you nothing to send out such a promotion, nor does it take much time to set up those lists in your e-mail.

DON'T JUST SHOW; YOU NEED TO SELL

A key principle of marketing is to know the competition and its weaknesses and to know your own strengths and make the most of those. When a prospect contacts you or comes to view an apartment, what's important is not just to show but to actively sell.

A failing of most owners and managers is they don't know what's out there nearly as well as the person who's looking for an apartment. You may have done a tour of all your competition when you were trying to figure out how you were going to renovate your building. Now, two years later, you've been operating a successful building and figure you could raise the rents by $25. However, your prospects have been out there looking at what is available right now. They are well versed in what is available and its asking price. By contrast, you may not be aware of what your competitors have been doing since you last visited them.

Even if you haven't visited the competition in a while—and you should have because the market is constantly changing—you can ask questions to draw out of your prospects what they have seen. "Hey, where else have you been? What did you like about that place? What didn't you like?" Their answers will give you an opening to sell the best features of your own apartments: "Yes, it's true they have put in a swimming pool, which you might use occasionally; but here, you will have new upgraded appliances in your apartment, which you will appreciate every single day." You can set up the kind of contrasts that persuade people to sign with you.

If people don't rent, it's very important to try to find out why. Give them a call, or send a survey. A lot of times, they'll ignore you or figure you're harassing them, but you can get some valuable feedback by simply explaining, "We're just doing a follow-up. We want to improve what we do, so we would appreciate your honest answer to these questions. What did you like and what didn't you like about the apartment? Why did you choose the apartment you ultimately rented?" If you ask such questions in a written survey, you might offer a $5 or $10 gift card for completing it, as we do when we survey new residents. You will get useful information. You may find out something that you didn't want to hear but needed to hear.

If you're the owner and you show your own apartments, have someone else do the follow-up. People tend to be less forthcoming with the person who showed them around. They'll tell more to a third party. You may be surprised at what you learn. "I really liked the place, but that person was just so rude," they might say. Or "I went in and they were eating lunch and didn't seem interested in even showing me the apartment." When you hear what turned a prospect off, you may discover that it is something you could readily control.

Marketing an apartment comes down to the principles of good salesmanship. Drill down to find out what people need and what will help them make the decision to choose you over someone else. If you can deflect whatever it is that might be persuading them to go elsewhere, you can steer business to your own apartments and further build your investment.

SET THE TONE FOR THE TOUR

You always want to make sure the property shows in its best light. Think about things that might influence a prospect's first impression of your property. Is there a better time of day to tour? Have you thought through the drive up to your property? Make a sincere effort to view your rental from the prospect's eyes, as though you are seeing it for the first time. How easy is it to find your property?

Should you add signage or maybe balloons and flowers for a more colorful and happy feeling? Remember, it is the feelings and experience you generate that will add the most value.

As you show the property and the rental unit, pay attention to items such as the positioning of your body during the tour. Give each room the feeling of maximum space. Practice demonstrating items such as under-cabinet lights. Open closets to show an organizing system. Incorporate as many visual and sensory elements as possible. Talk about how the light comes through the windows. If there's a view, draw attention to it. Do things in a memorable way

🏠 *Remember, it is the feelings and experience you generate that will add the most value.*

Avoid talking too much. You want to establish rapport with your prospects. But your primary goal is to make them experience the apartment or home, not just see it. You want to involve them. They won't lease until they can see themselves living there. And don't forget to invite your prospects to lease!

USING YOUR MARKETING TOOLS

As we discussed earlier, thinking through the rental experience and creating a good one is key to getting better tenants, higher rents, and shorter vacancy times. Many times, your first contact with a prospective tenant is either a phone call or an e-mail. You want to be ready to respond appropriately, depending on the mode of communication. Sometimes, that means creating an enticing flyer, in advance, that you can e-mail to prospects. This helps sell your property and gets them to want to visit. Your goal in that first contact, whether by phone, e-mail, or some other medium, is to set an appointment to tour. You always want to book appointments. Saying, "We're open from 9 a.m. to 5 p.m." does not help you get them in. The tone needs to set a feeling of personal service and also a feeling that the vacant unit will go quickly, so an appointment is necessary.

Many times, I will book appointments very tightly together, or sometimes, I book two at the same time. When the prospects see others also looking, it helps reinforce the sense of urgency and the fact that there is competition out there.

Remember the show. Include signs of welcome, such as a nice welcome mat, balloons, flowers, and so on. Depending on the size of your community, you might have anything from a simple presentation binder, which includes testimonial letters from satisfied residents, to a short video they can watch that will get them wanting to rent at your property. You should have something they can take home with them. This could be something as simple as a flyer that lists the features and benefits of the rental and the neighborhood, or it can be a more extravagant package that includes floor plans and other information. Business is theater, especially sales and customer service. Remember: don't sell price; sell value. The prospects you want are selective. They can afford to look at many places.

YOUR SCREENING PROCESS STARTS THE MOMENT PROSPECTS ARRIVE (AND EVEN BEFORE)

You've done a great job of attracting prospects to your rental. You've set the tone for the showing, and the property is looking its best. You are selling them on the wonderful, unique attributes of your rental. However, now you must also start the process of screening out people so you can find the best resident for you. As you tour the property with them, you also screen them. This is the key to getting the right resident.

If you are the one showing the unit, ask questions of your potential applicants, including:

- How many people will be staying at the property?

- What kind of pets do you have? (This is better than asking them whether or not they have pets.)

- Why are you moving? (Do they speak poorly of their former landlord? Do they talk about a mold problem?)

- How long are you planning to stay? (Since turnover is your largest expense, long term is usually preferred.)

- When I contact your previous landlord/management, what will they say about you? (Listen carefully to what they say.)

You will want to make mental notes of what they say (or, if you get a chance, write them down). Compare this to what you see on the rental application when it is returned.

THE RENTAL APPLICATION

Your rental application is one of the best tools you have to screen tenants. Yes, it needs to contain the basic information including name, date of birth, Social Security number, and so on, but it should also ask questions that help you determine whether or not this applicant will be a suitable tenant for your rental. These questions might include:

O   How long will you live here?

O   Is the total move-in amount available now?

O   Have you previously broken a lease?

O   How many evictions have been filed on you? (Notice the difference from "Have you ever been evicted?")

O   What type of animals do you have?

O   If your application is approved, list the people who will be living with you.

O   Is there anyone living with you now who will not be living with you at this property?

O   How did you find this home? (This is a marketing question.)

You want some behavioral-based questions on the application. Some of these will be similar to the questions asked on your tour. Others might include:

O   Have you had any recurring problems with the property at your last home or apartment?

O   Have you ever been asked to move?

Include an "Other Comments and Explanations" section on the application. This section can be used by the applicant to detail some items. You may get rants about prior landlords. Proceed with caution.

Let the applicants know that their application will be considered along with others. Advise them that it is very important to fill out the application as completely as possible. Inform them that they need to turn the application in as quickly as possible to avoid the risk of losing the rental to competing prospects.

Make sure your application has a spot where the applicant certifies that the application is true and correct and that if they misrepresented the facts, they will be disqualified.

When you receive the completed application, do a quick review. Make sure all items are filled out. Make sure the applicant's handwriting is legible. Clarify any portions you can't decipher. Verify the information on the application by comparing it with information on the driver's license or other documents. Look for inconsistencies or red flags.

Your application and screening process is key. This is one of the most important, yet undervalued, areas in managing rental property. Too many owners and managers are so focused on getting that vacancy filled quickly to the first marginally qualified applicant that they don't really pay attention to what is best for the property in the long term.

We found added value in targeting the gray areas: people with weaker FICO scores may still make good tenants. Anyone can rent to a person who fits some computer algorithm's screening model. Added value may lie in those who don't make a clean cut in the other areas.

Make sure your rental application is properly worded and legal. Your application is your best weapon for screening out potential problem residents.

FRAUD SCREENING GUIDELINES

With the advent of the Internet, tenant screening has become both easier (you can verify physical addresses and other data quickly) and harder (there are now entire industries providing fake identity and background information). You must not accept everything you receive at face value. It is your job to assume fraud and double-check everything. Simply running a credit report and relying on a credit score is just not good enough anymore.

Make sure the person on the identification is the person seated across the desk from you, not simply someone who looks similar. Does the address on the ID (and the date of the ID) line up with what has been put down on the application form? After the application has been completed, review it for completeness. If something looks odd, ask questions.

Most larger businesses and most banks have online capabilities for paystubs or for bank statements. Have your applicant log on at the computer in the leasing office so you can verify information rather than accept printouts. It is too easy to get fake copies on the Internet these days.

At a minimum, check the math on the paystubs or review paycheck numbers. We've had people submit what were supposedly copies of paychecks received weeks apart, yet the checks were, literally, in sequence (as if no checks had been printed to anyone else in the interim). In the same way, if they work for a small business, the check numbers should not jump by several hundred in just a few weeks.

It is easy to buy manufactured pay stubs and other employment information on the Internet. Cross-check phone numbers and other company information to make sure they are legitimate.

Are there any typos or misspellings? Do any lines not quite line up (as if someone did a cut and paste job)?

Check the name and address of their workplace through a quick Google search. Check reverse directories (for phone numbers) if you can. Google the phone number. If the business is a real business, it will usually show up. Cell phone numbers will not.

When verifying employment, call the main number and ask for the person the applicant claims is her supervisor rather than calling the number directly. It could easily be a friend's cell phone number.

Use Google Maps to view the structures applicants claim are their current home, their current workplace, and so on. We once found an abandoned warehouse as the location of a claimed employer. Another time it was an empty lot.

Does their credit report have nothing on it? Unless they are just starting out, this is rare. Check with your screening provider to see if there could be something wrong.

Ask for written employment and rental verification information. Check the handwriting on the form and compare it to the application. Verifying previous landlords can be one of the tougher things to do. Start with verifying ownership of the address they claim to live at and so on.

Always ask to see original documents. Do not accept photocopies.

SCREENING POST APPLICATION

Read and analyze the information you receive. The object of screening is not to get completed forms. The object is to use that data to determine whether or not that prospect will make a good tenant at one of your rentals.

As you look the application over, determine whether the information seems to make sense. When verifying residency or employment, see if you can find phone numbers online and whether or not they match what you were given. You can do searches on Facebook by e-mail address. You can view buildings on Google Maps.

Have a checklist to award points based on answers. This will help protect you if an applicant claims discrimination. Remember you are looking for more than ability to pay. Other problems that can come up include unauthorized occupants, drugs, nuisance issues, and other nonfinancial data. While these are the hardest items to verify, it is critical you at least attempt to get verification from the applicant's previous landlord.

Some questions to ask an applicant's previous landlord include:

- Did this applicant live at the address given, and can you confirm dates and rental amounts?

- Why did this applicant leave your property?

- Did this applicant give a proper thirty-day notice of intent to vacate?

- Was the security deposit returned in full?

- Were any three-day or thirty-day notices ever served on this applicant during tenancy?

- Would you rent to this person again?

Don't assume everything on the application is true unless you have verified it. Beware of information that is impossible to verify. Also, in evaluating the application, always ask yourself how likely it is you'll get paid if something goes wrong.

TALK TO YOUR PROSPECTS

Modern technology has made it possible to attract and screen tenants without ever meeting them. This is not necessarily a good thing.

Whether or not you are the one showing the apartment where you can actually meet prospects, you can call them up while reviewing their application and ask a few questions. They are going to be occupying a portion of your personal wealth. You should at least get a sense of them. You can use the opportunity to review certain items on their application and get some explanations or answers to questions.

You can mix in some additional screening questions such as:

- Have you had any recurring problems with the property at your last home or apartment?

- Have you had disagreements with your last manager or landlord?

Talking to them also gives you a chance to resell the benefits of your unit. Use the phone. It is a powerful screening tool. Take good notes. If it is not written down, it never happened. Taking good notes will help protect you later should any prospects claim discrimination in how you selected them. Send the message that you are an active property owner or manager. Communicate your commitment to do a thorough and complete screening of all your applicants.

The importance of proper tenant attraction and screening cannot be overemphasized. Done properly, it is your single best tool to ensure that your properties will be more profitable, you'll have lower expenses, and your life will be easier. Your goal is not just to fill your vacancy fast but also to fill it with an ideal resident. Doing this right will have a positive impact on you for many years to come.

CHAPTER 7

MAINTENANCE, UTILITIES, AND TURNOVER

Why Focusing on These Three Areas
Will Yield You More Than Any Others

When I was in college, my dormitory had a steam heat system that seemed to operate with a mind of its own—and seemed to have no recognition of human comfort. The system would crank out so much heat that the students would open their windows wide to keep their rooms at a semicomfortable temperature. The furnace would be running full force in a building with half the windows open.

We had a similar issue in a building here in Oakland when we took over its operation. Half the tenants had their windows open because they were too hot. The other half barely got warm enough.

We soon learned that the heat for the entire building was run by a thermostat located in one apartment. Whoever had set that up—it was probably because it had been a former manager's apartment—put the thermostat in an apartment that tended to be chilly. Everyone else was boiling and opening windows, thereby giving the owner a huge gas bill every month. All we did was move the thermostat to one of the mid-warm to slightly warm units, and 30 to 40 percent of the heating bill went away instantly.

At other times, when we have had people wasting fuel and even tampering with the thermostat, we put a clear, locked box over the control. We told the tenants that, in an emergency, they could call us. That solved the problem. Or you can install a thermostat that you program to the desired temperature so that the tenant cannot change it. You can also install thermostats that measure the outdoor temperature so that the furnace won't come on unless the temperature drops to the degree you designate.

Such easy solutions demonstrate how readily a landlord can control certain expenses. Expense reports contain numerous categories including administration, marketing and advertising, property taxes, and insurance. You control every category to some degree. There are ways to lower your insurance rates, for example. Property taxes can be adjusted.

The three easiest to control, however, with the quickest impact on your bottom line, are your utility costs, your maintenance costs, and your turnover costs. In this chapter, we'll take a look at what you can do in those three main categories.

UTILITIES

The first question to ask about utilities is this: can costs be transferred to the tenants? That's the easiest way to control your utility expenses. When the tenants are actually paying the bill and see how the costs affect their personal budget, it makes a huge difference in their usage habits.

In many cases, transferring utility costs to the tenants through separate metering is expensive because of the way the building is wired or piped. A common solution, in states that allow it, is called a resident utility billing system (RUBS). There are companies that do utility billing using standard formulas based on hundreds of thousands of apartments. Let's say it's water use. You have ten apartments in a building, with different numbers of occupants, bedrooms, and square footage. The company, using those variables, calculates that 9 percent of the total usage should be attributed to this apartment, and 11 percent to that one, and so on.

It's not an exact billing, because a tenant who goes away for a month and comes back might say, "I wasn't even using water. Why am I paying?" Of course your answer is, "If we didn't use this allocation system, which is the fairest we could come up with, you'd be paying more because we would have to just build it into the rent." Getting a bill helps reduce use because people see the issue. It builds in responsibility for people who, otherwise, can resort to slamming it to the landlord.

Technology offers numerous solutions to help monitor and control utility costs. There are little meters that you can install at point of use. We had a building where the supply line to the toilet had a meter, as did the vanity, as did the hot water and the cold water line to the kitchen sink, and so on. The meters are built into the supply lines and send a signal to a collector, which sends it to the billing company. If a landlord is bored at 2 a.m., he could even check the systems on his computer: "Oh my God, there's a toilet leak in apartment ten!" The landlord can see whether water is running and tenants aren't reporting it. Experienced landlords know what that's like: "Oh, yeah, it's been

🏠 Technology offers numerous solutions to help monitor and control utility costs.

like that for five months," the tenant says. "We just didn't get around to calling."

Electricity is easier than water pipes both to separately meter and submeter. Pulling a wire in a wall and hooking up a meter to it is so much easier than doing so with pipes. The meters are placed near the subpanel. It is very accurate. If the tenant is not using power, the meter doesn't run. It only runs when electricity is flowing. The meters get a read for each apartment, which sends the information to a collector, which sends it to the billing company, similar to the way in which water meter readings are handled. The landlord gets a single electric bill to reconcile, divvying it up among the tenants according to how much power they used that month. Then the billing company sends out separate bills of various amounts to the tenants.

That can be done for electricity, water usage, and, in theory, for gas usage. Some states don't allow it for gas. If you opt for a resident utility billing service, it generally costs the owner about $4 per unit per month. Some owners pass this cost to the residents. We choose not to do so, because we don't think tenants should pay for us to have the right to bill them.

The service substantially cuts down the cost. Even if you encounter some collection and compliance issues where utilities are concerned, you can, ultimately, take the costs from the deposit. I recommend you adjust your lease to include a utility addendum that spells out tenants' responsibilities and how payments will be applied (first to outstanding utility bills and then to rent).

You don't want to get so frugal that you become the penny-pinching landlord who forgets about marketability and tenant comfort for the sake of savings. Today's technology gives us the ability to save in other ways.

One way to reduce your electric costs, after all, would be to eliminate lighting in common areas. That's not the smartest move. Otherwise, you could turn out some of the lights or install fluorescents or even LEDs. You could put them on timers or use photocells. Just be sure to adjust the timers regularly, and don't put a photocell near a streetlight or the apartment lights will go out when the streetlight goes on. It may make sense to replace the fixtures. Many utilities offer incentives or rebates, even free energy-efficient light fixtures. You might want to check for any incentives that are available to you.

In controlling heating and air conditioning expenses, insulation, obviously, is a big factor. You may have a high up-front cost, but given that rates are rising, you can save. If certain apartments get unusually hot, you can add awnings or even plant shade trees.

A major water user is the toilet, which typically accounts for 45 percent of the water use of an apartment. Tenants often don't know when toilets are leaking. That's why a micrometer on the supply line is a good idea, or you can schedule regular inspections. Have your maintenance guy go through all the units and do the dye test: you put a little dye in the tank and see if it goes into the bowl.

One way to see if you're having a problem is to check the usage on your bill. As a rough measure, the average use should be about a hundred gallons per person per day. If you're at two hundred gallons a person a day, something is leaking.

Investing a couple extra dollars in a slightly more expensive flush arm for your toilet tank could bring you big savings over time, and that ties into the issue of quality. I have a horror story about this. Years ago, our water utility company was trying to get people to replace their standard five-gallon flush toilets with the newer, low-flow, three-and-a-half-gallon toilets. They offered to pay for the new toilets and install them for free. We signed up for that program. The utility company installed new, water-saving toilets in a twenty-two-unit apartment building. But the next month, our water bill didn't go down. In fact, the next month, it actually was higher than it had been with the "water guzzlers." It turned out that the replacement toilets were so poorly made that tenants had to flush them two or three times. We ended up with the big expense of ripping out all those cheap toilets and replacing them with higher-quality, low-flow toilets.

Another utility to consider is trash collection. In most cases, you're charged by the size of the container. It doesn't matter if it's a cubic yard of garbage or a cubic yard of air, you're still being charged for it. You really want to look at whether your trash bins and cans are being filled with empty boxes that have not been broken down. Are you overpaying, essentially? Is the garbage receptacle two-thirds full when they take it away or is it overflowing? Figure out the proper use for your tenants.

Once again, the principle of small things adding up applies here. Even minor savings on bills add up, particularly when multiplied over many apartments. If you can save just 10 percent more through such efficiencies, you can easily double the profit on your bottom line. Lenders look at utility costs as fixed items. Many buyers do as well. If you're going for a new loan or if you're selling a building, both buyers and lenders look at all the line items. You're going to have your utility line item, your insurance line item, and your maintenance line item when trying to determine the value of the property. Although they may put in their own numbers for insurance or maintenance costs, most people mistakenly assume utilities are what they are. The truth is utilities are extremely variable. If you can get your utility costs down, you will immediately be able to get a better loan or better sales price.

If you have decided you want to separate the utilities and get individual tenants to pay their fair share, then it makes sense to accomplish that change while you are doing a major rehab of the building. As part of planning your rehab, this is a key thing to think about. Again, if there's a way you can transfer costs to the residents, you'll immediately not only increase your cash flow but significantly add to the value of your building. So if the walls are open anyway, that's a good time to consider submeter installation because you will have easier access to pipes and wires. You might also add a washer/dryer hook-up in a unit, which would add immediate value by increasing demand among renters.

MAINTENANCE

Maintenance is another expense the landlord can easily control. While some expenses are inevitable, you can do some things proactively to help keep your costs down, much of which has to do with choosing quality products and service so you save money in the long run.

Most of the home improvement stores are geared toward homeowners. They sell faucets and other products that look nice and are certainly marketable but do not hold up to the wear and tear tenants can put on your rental property. You're going to find yourself spending a lot in labor costs to replace them every few years. It's the same story with certain carpets, countertops, and other materials. If they're in your own home they're going to last because you take extra care of them, but in rental units, some people just seem to find a way to destroy things.

That's why a landlord should look at products and materials that are longer lasting and designed to be durable. Earlier, I mentioned that you could use tile instead of vinyl in a bathroom because it wouldn't cost that much more but would make the bathroom more bombproof to tenants. There are many examples of how you can save that way.

Labor cost is also important. Your job will typically be 60 percent or more in labor and under 40 percent materials. That's why it pays to keep common supplies and materials on site. You don't want to take an hour of some guy's time to run to Home Depot to buy lightbulbs or washers.

You can also save by standardizing. If you have a twenty-unit apartment building, you really should try to use the same faucets, the same refrigerators, and the same light fixtures because when things break, you don't need an infinite number of parts in your inventory. You have the same things for all your tenants, and you offer the same upgrades.

We do this for a lot of different materials and products. For example, after our bad experience with the free toilets, we researched which ones would take abuse and serve our purposes best. We didn't get the $75 toilet, but we didn't get the $400 toilet either. We found one that was around $200, and it had a powerful flush. That toilet became *the* toilet for us. Its internal mechanisms were all of better quality, designed for abuse. The better the quality, the longer the fixture will last. You will have fewer service calls, and if you buy the same fixtures for many of your apartments, you will realize the price savings that come with the economy of standardization and interchangeable parts.

If you're buying to flip and sell, you might take a different approach, but landlords usually buy with the intent to hold and rent. It's best to think long term. For example, I recently decided to replace the flooring in some apartments with luxury vinyl tile that looks like wood planks. The tenants think it's hardwood. One tenant even asked me how to keep the wood floor looking good. I had to explain that it wasn't wood and that waxing it would work just fine. The flooring makes the apartments look more luxurious and spacious. That project cost me double what I would have paid for a typical vinyl and carpet treatment, but it will last much longer (and allow me to rent the unit for more money).

Carpets last five years in apartments, on average—but some last only a year or so. Tenants tend to slosh their coffee and scatter crumbs. Providing them with a vacuum helps, but don't expect them to take care of the carpet as you would if it were your own. By choosing a material that costs more but will certainly last longer than five years, you are saving money. It comes down to thinking about your long-term savings over your short-term savings. It's a good idea to plan your operating budget over five years, and after one year, see where savings are possible.

Make a checklist of routine maintenance tasks that must be done. That's important. If you go to Jiffy Lube for an oil change, they'll put your car through their twelve-point checklist. They will invariably find something besides the oil that should be changed. We do that for apartments. For move-ins, we come up with a checklist of common items we need to make sure work. If we have these regular services packaged and done at the time of a new move-in, we won't have to do maintenance on them in an occupied apartment.

The checklist includes a wide range of items including putting new batteries in the smoke detectors, checking all the burners on the stove, replacing faucet washers, and so on. By doing them all at once and knowing that you have a fresh run for the next tenant, you save yourself money. To make an emergency maintenance call is always more expensive than just having things working well from the start.

The checklist can spare you a nightmare. A tenant we evicted once stuffed dozens of tampons down a toilet just before she vacated the premises. Our maintenance crew didn't flush the toilet as part of the regular procedure in turning over the unit. The first time the new tenant flushed the toilet, we had a major flood. The maintenance man would have known to immediately turn off the shutoff valve at the base of the toilet if he had only checked. Instead, the toilet ran and ran until water was running down the walls of the apartment below, causing over $1,000 in damage. It was sabotaged by a tenant bent on getting even with the landlord, but the problem could have been easily caught had we had the checklist procedure in place.

A landlord needs to be savvy about maintenance issues but does not necessarily need to be the do-it-yourself type. Always be aware of how much your time is worth. It comes down to saying, "Do I paint this apartment? The paint only costs me $150, but it takes me two days to do this. Do I hire that painter who will do it for $250 in labor costs?" The question becomes one of evaluating what two days of your time are worth and other things you could be doing with that time. You might consciously say, "I don't have the money. I'm going to do it myself," or you might realize that your time might be better spent doing something else.

If you could market the apartment and get it rented more quickly, rather than spend your time painting it and doing the maintenance, you might end up covering your entire cost of paying someone else to paint it. You need to consider your opportunity cost. How much money are you not making by spending your time that way?

You certainly want to perform an annual review on your suppliers and contracts. We tend to hire landscapers and painters, especially if we have a larger portfolio, and we use them each year. Over time, there may be a little cost creep. Are the people you hired still the best for your money? Are you getting a package deal? Are they doing as good a job as on the first day they started? Some people are so busy trying to get new jobs that once you become their regular client, the attention to detail starts waning as they focus on the next client. It might be time to get a quote from somebody else.

In your annual review, ask yourself whether you still need the service. Do you need it with the same scope and frequency as when it was first contracted? Could it be done with less cost, or better, by another vendor, perhaps one who will give you a break for volume?

Don't replace items that should be repaired. There are products to make cosmetic repairs to countertops and tubs that get scratched, for example. You can use dye to cover stains in carpeting. Such measures may not be perfect but certainly can buy you another tenancy or two before you have to spend the big money and replace the entire item. The flip side of that, however, is that you shouldn't repair items that should be replaced. Let's say you spend $150 to repair an existing stove and end up with a stove that does indeed work but is still ugly and eight years old. For $300 you could have bought a brand new stove and received the marketing and warranty value that comes with that. Sometimes, it makes more sense to replace rather than repair.

Also, don't pay for repairs for which your residents should be charged. If someone's repeatedly clogging the toilet with items that shouldn't be there, such as their cell phone, and you're paying Roto-

Rooter to clear it out all the time, you need to charge the tenant. Some landlords fear they will lose tenants that way. But sometimes you just have to charge. If you rent a car, the attendant will walk around it, checking its condition, and when you bring it back, you will be charged if it's dented. Consider the circumstances. You don't want to lose your good residents for inadvertent damage. But repeated abuse definitely needs to be charged back. Sometimes you just say, "You pay half and I'll pay half." That's better than not charging anything.

You might consider a deductible for service calls. For example, the tenant would be responsible for the first $75 of any service call. It can cut way down on minor calls for nonsensical reasons. However, the downside is that tenants might not report problems and might let them get worse because they don't want to pay anything. You have to find the right balance.

Educating your tenants about maintenance is a good way to cut down on costs. You don't want to be doing maintenance in the first place. Provide your tenants with a list of frequently asked questions about maintenance and what they reasonably could do themselves. You don't want to hire your tenants to be maintenance people, but it helps to give them an orientation and point things out, such as if the garbage disposal gets clogged, there's this little red button on the bottom that they press to get it going again. Or there are these things called GFI outlets. The little button in the middle sometimes pops because it's overloaded. If it is pressed again, it can be reset. Or that box in their closet contains what is called circuit breakers, and here's how they work.

You'd be amazed. Most people don't know some of those basics. You would think people know that if the toilet is overflowing, they must turn the shut-off valve behind the toilet. But many don't even know the shut-off valve exists. I even had a tenant who called the fire department about a wall heater in the apartment. The tenant was from a Latin American country and wasn't used to having heaters. One chilly day, the heater in the apartment came on. The tenant, thinking the wall was on fire, called the fire department.

Even worse can be tenants who think they know everything but do not. You can advise tenants on what to check in an emergency, but you should never give them authority, or hire them, to do work or repairs. If tenants say, "Hey, we can't pay the $800 rent this month. Can we paint the apartment instead or paint the vacant apartment instead to help work it off?" you have to say no. When you say yes, I'll tell you what inevitably happens. Pretty soon, they are looking for another job from you and can never pay the rent. When you confront them about not paying, they say, "Well you didn't have any work for me this month. How do you expect me to be able to pay you?"

It can seem that when you do someone a favor, it can come back to bite you. If you do give someone a rent credit for doing something such as cleaning the hallways on a regular basis, just have a really clear understanding of expectations regarding their duties and what you expect for the rent credit. But I never give free rent. I always want tenants to pay something and get something back. Even if it's a rent discount, they need to still have the action of paying something. Otherwise, they forget that they are getting compensation. They start thinking, "Why am I doing all this work?" That's why it's important that anything of that nature should be covered in a clearly written agreement.

TURNOVER

The third expense category that can readily be reduced is turnover. The easiest way to cut down your turnover costs is to not have turnover in the first place. It could be as simple as that.

Studies and surveys have shown that over two-thirds of all turnover is controllable. Why do people move? The answers tend to be things such as: the maintenance takes too long; the maintenance is not done very well; the manager is rude; the apartment costs are too high. That last reason is subtle. It really means the tenants feel they are not getting enough value for what they're paying. Sometimes people move because they have been relocated on the job, or they're having a baby and need more than a studio apartment, but the truth is that most of the reasons for tenants moving out are within your control.

If you want to cut down on your turnover costs, cut down your turnover. If you want to cut down your turnover, you need to do the things I am advocating in this book; attend to customer service, and stay in touch with people so they don't feel ignored.

You also want to look at whom you're bringing in. When reviewing rental applications, one of the things we look for is how long prospects tend to stay at places. If they move every year, there's a good chance they're going to move next year. If you've got prospects who live four years at this place and six years at that place, there's a good chance they're going to be four years at your place or more. Now, granted, your apartment could be the one that changes that pattern for them, but certainly, the duration of previous tenancies is something you want to consider.

Studies have shown that the typical loss for every turnover is well over the monthly rent for that unit, perhaps several times the rent. You're spending $1,500 to $3,000 per unit, sometimes more. You have to factor in your lost rent during the vacancy, your marketing time and energy, all the times you have to show an apartment to attract someone, and the cost of actually getting an apartment ready, whether it's painting, carpet cleaning, or something more extensive. And you should also consider the opportunity cost: the time you're spending trying to rent the apartment is time you'd be spending doing something else if you didn't have the turnover in the first place.

There will always be some turnover. What's important is to have strategies in place that will reduce the costs. They include having an adequate security deposit and a thorough move-in and move-out checklist. Your checklist can include photos or video of any damage to help assess charges. It's good to have a list of charges for specific damages so you have a clear understanding with the tenant. If the tenant has agreed to that list in advance, you can avoid the squabbling.

A major way to reduce costs, however, is to avoid letting the apartment sit vacant for weeks on end. Efficient scheduling and planning will help you get new tenants in quickly. Good marketing goes far in reducing turnover costs. If you have a building that has several apartments with the same floor plan, you can arrange to show prospects a nicely decorated one while work is being completed on the vacant one.

Good marketing goes far in reducing turnover costs.

You should line up your contracts and your vendors and have everything ready to go as soon as you get access to the apartment. Usually, people give you a thirty-day notice so you already know ahead of time that they're moving out. You need to visit the unit and see if there's anything that might require ordering ahead of time, especially if you're doing some renovations. For example, as each apartment turns, you might have decided that you will get rid of those cheap, hollow-core, flush doors and put in nice Masonite, raised-panel doors. You likely will need a few weeks to order those in advance, so don't delay. You want to be ready to install them right after the move-out.

In the spirit of keeping the tenant happy, some landlords even offer a discount to prevent turnover. They lower the rent for the contract extension or for part of the contract extension. Whether you should do that will, again, depend on the ultimate cost. Ask yourself what it will cost you to give this tenant something versus what it will cost to rip up the apartment and redo it. You may decide on a discount, but I advocate giving tenants an upgrade. If they say, "Well we're thinking of moving. We're having a little trouble affording it," you might reason that you could give them a $25 temporary rent reduction per month because it would cost you $2,000 if they moved out. Remember, however, that doing so will lower your property value. If you are going to be selling or refinancing, that's a major consideration. However, if you're planning to hold for a while and their situation is temporary, due to a job issue or the economy, a reduction is certainly something to consider.

If you think the tenants' real issue is that they think the apartment is getting too expensive for the amenities you offer, you should consider how you might satisfy and retain them. Carpet cleaning can work wonders; it costs you $75, and you get a new lease. Perhaps the tenant wants you to replace the stove, repaint an accent wall, or do some other upgrades.

You want to do a thorough cleaning between tenants anyway. Take care of all those minor repairs that can become big repairs if you don't deal with them: the caulking, the nail holes, and the leaks. That's why you need to keep your apartments in good shape as much as you can during tenancy, as it reduces your costs on turnover. Make sure the tenants are keeping the apartment in reasonable condition and not turning it into a mess. Otherwise, four years later, when they move out, you could face a surprise costing many thousands of dollars.

If you stay with your tenants along the way, you can prevent that. And it's important that you stay with your tenants in a lot of ways, not just to monitor how well they're taking care of the apartment. You need to do your part to take good care of them. In the long run, that's the best way to reduce turnover and increase your profits.

CHAPTER 8

RECLAIMING A PROBLEM PROPERTY

Adding Value through Solving
Other People's Problems

Four tenants had taken over the building by the time we were called in to clean things up. Traffic was coming and going at all hours of the day and night. Clearly, someone was dealing drugs.

Most of the tenants in this forty-unit property were not involved and, it appeared, didn't want to be. But those four had affected the tone for the entire building. Most of the good tenants tried to stay inside their apartments. The place had become run-down, and the residents stayed away from the common areas and didn't use the amenities. They just didn't feel comfortable.

In response, we first gated the community so that drivers actually had to call in before they could enter. Then we focused on getting rid of those four people—and eventually, they were out.

After the immediate problem was resolved, we found that we had a whole new level of problem tenants. These were people whom we had tolerated earlier, even though they were seminuisances. They weren't drug dealers, but they blasted their music and paid their rent late. In comparison with drug dealers, however, they had seemed like saints, but it was now time to crack down on them too.

After that, the remaining residents remarkably became good tenants. I have found that if a building has 10 percent good tenants and 10 percent bad ones, the other 80 percent could go either way, depending on the tone of the building. We had people who only became good tenants once they saw that we were kicking out the problem people. There's a lesson there on human nature. Most people are followers, and they will follow good or they will follow bad.

It's an axiom of the business that your tenants reflect your building. Whenever we would go into a building and start cleaning it up, we would also try to figure out which tenants were the problems. What I found was that in, say, a thirty-unit building, there were typically only two or three tenants who really had go, even though quite a few others would be nothing to brag about. I saw the pattern: Once the bad ones were gone, many of their followers improved. However, some of those whom we had previously tolerated would now seem to be the bad ones. Usually, that would happen in a couple of waves.

IS IT WORTH THE EFFORT?

When you're considering upgrading a rental property or buying one that needs work, the first thing you need to ask yourself is this: is it even worth doing? A lot of properties, frankly, don't offer a lot of upside potential. You also need to ask yourself what you can do differently. How can you change the way the property is managed? What can you do differently in the way it is marketed and in how it is positioned from a design standpoint? Basically, you are assessing how you can change the existing management's strategies to make the property successful.

Your first impression is important when you go up to the property:

- What do you notice?

- What do you think of the landscaping if there is any?

- Does maintenance seem up to par?

- Are the surroundings attractive or barren?

- Is the signage adequate?

- Is there fencing on the property?

Try to make notes on your first impression or on your first few visits because once you are familiar with the place, you lose that sense of how it feels from a prospective tenant's perspective; you now have the landlord's perspective. Try to keep fresh in your mind the things that a prospect would perceive. You need to do a cool, unemotional analysis of whether you will be able to make changes to maximize the property's value in the marketplace, including the amount of demand for the type of unit you would be offering.

One of those changes—in many ways, the easiest—might be in the nature of the tenancy. A lot of times, you can get a bargain on a property because the tenants have taken over and the owner's given up. Even if he hasn't quite given up, he's hurting economically because tenants are not paying rent. Some have questionable characters. You, as the new owner coming in, have to figure out how to get rid of these people.

AVOID THE LEGAL SYSTEM IF POSSIBLE

Even when you eventually win with the legal system, it's a slow process, and you can lose all your good people while waiting to have your day in court.

Let's say one of your tenants is a nuisance, dealing drugs or blasting music. You serve that tenant a notice and you say, in effect, "Hey, if you don't get your act together, we're going to evict you." The tenant doesn't change and you finally file for unlawful detainer.

By the time it gets to court, especially if the tenant uses some delay tactics, you could be forty-five or sixty days out. Most of your other tenants have been dealing with this problem for a while, and even though you are finally taking action, they're just tired of it. They're going to move when their lease ends and, frankly, in many cases, they'll break their lease. While you're slowly dealing with this problem through the legal system, the four tenants who live around the problem tenant's unit all move. Now you have a bigger problem.

Sometimes you can pay people to move. You don't want to make this your general policy because word gets around, but it might make sense to just buy them off. We'd go up to people and say, "Look, if I file an eviction on you, I will win. It's going to cost me $700 in legal fees. Frankly, per our lease, you're going to be responsible for paying me back when we win. It doesn't help you or me to get in this battle. So here's the deal: if you move out by next weekend, I'll give you the $700." It comes down to paying a lawyer or paying the tenant. The tactic often works.

Other times, I've simply said, "Look, you're going to lose your deposit when you move out, so I'll tell you what. I'll give you your deposit back if you move out next weekend." That works just as well. Depending on the situation, you have to decide how much you are willing to spend.

Also, you can warn tenants that they will have a hard time finding any other place to rent if an eviction is on their record and anyone calls for references. It gives them pause for thought. It's in their best interest to keep this out of the legal system so that they can rent elsewhere.

DOCUMENTING YOUR CASE

You should try to deal with troublesome tenants before eviction by negotiating with them, but some problems are incurable and the issue becomes getting these people out as soon as possible.

🏠 *It's in your interest to take care of things with all due speed.*

The key is documentation, and it's easier to do these days. Any time you go to court, it's a "he-said, she-said" drama, especially if you end up going to small claims court. Many tenants have become aware that landlords often do not keep good records.

Smart landlords will do a walk-through of the apartment to document its condition before a tenant moves in. Take photos or video. It's easy and cheap to do these days. Then, when the tenant moves out, you have your evidence if he has trashed the place or claims that those bare wires were always there instead of a light fixture.

If you have inherited a bad tenant from a previous landlord and lack good records, you should set up a unit-by-unit inspection. Walk the property. If you see code deficiencies that you know will be a problem, you need to spend a little money to address them. You will not be able to get rid of a problem tenant unless you can show that you have kept your side of the deal. If you do go into a tenant's unit and notice that someone has torn off a light fixture, you need to install one before you can do an eviction.

Sometimes, when you take over a property, it looks fine, but two months later, a tenant who hasn't been paying rent will show up in court with pictures of holes in the wall and electrical wires dangling from the ceiling and say, "This is how we have to live!" Again, if you do an initial unit-by-unit inspection and note whether the conditions are okay, you will have a record that should satisfy the court. It's not as good as photographic evidence, but because you inspected each and every unit, you have demonstrated that you were not targeting any particular tenant.

Tenants can be very adept at doing their own documenting. The one day when the garbage doesn't get picked up and it's overflowing with trash all over the place, they will be out there taking pictures. Then, in court, they will say, "Look at the trash. It looks like this all the time," and it may have overflowed only once. Just know that you have to be prepared for these things.

It's almost as if you have to think the worst of people—and they certainly can be difficult at times, particularly during evictions. One way to counter such claims is to frequently take photographs of the garbage area, laundry room, and other common areas, showing them to be clean and tidy. Also, remember that garbage companies often charge extra for days when they have a particularly bad mess to clean up, so you can produce your bills and show that only one of them was a little higher because that was the one day when the garbage overflowed.

DOING WHAT IS REASONABLE

Tenants who don't want to pay their rent may invoke the word *uninhabitable* as they try to make their case in court. "They just won't fix the dishwasher," they may say and claim they cannot be expected to live in such an apartment. It's hard to prove that an apartment is not habitable. Just because some issue goes unattended doesn't mean the place is uninhabitable. A dirty carpet does not make it uninhabitable, for example. Nor do roaches. Your duty as landlord is to try to solve the problem. You can't guarantee that you can eradicate pests, because the tenants themselves may bring them in. You can call the pest control company. That's your legal responsibility. Whether the pests all vanish is not your responsibility. A tenant may never clean her apartment and be living life in filth, but you are not the one to clean it up.

Mold is a common tenant complaint. A tenant may claim your building is the source of the problem. Yet when you walk into the apartment, it's obvious someone has just showered, no windows are open, and it feels as if you're in the Amazon rainforest. The tenant points to a little spot of mold on the bathroom ceiling, apparently oblivious to matters of cleanliness and ventilation, and swears it must be coming from inside the walls.

When we get a mold complaint and cannot convince the tenant of the need to clean and ventilate, we may take a hole saw drill bit, the kind you use when installing a doorknob, and cut a two-inch circle in the bathroom wallboard. We show the tenant the piece we cut out, establishing that the wallboard is dry on the backside of the wall. That means that any mold problem has arisen from inside the apartment, not within the walls or structure. Then we replace the circle and patch and paint, a quick and easy repair. Mold complaint resolved.

The very tenants who claim you leased them an uninhabitable apartment may themselves be creating a health and safety condition at your building because of how they live. The pests and other problems they invite will eventually infect others. Your reliable tenants will get fed up and move out. Good communication helps. If your good tenants understand that you are working to eradicate a problem, they will have more patience. They'll work with you if they know that you're responding to them and that you are doing something specific.

If you have established strategies for dealing with common tenant issues, and particularly with those that tend to come up in eviction court, then you should fare well. But sometimes the best way to deal with an unreasonable resident is to just say good-bye at the end of the lease. That's part of improving the overall tenancy in your building.

LITIGIOUS LAWYERS

Several years ago, we had to deal with a tenant attorney who went around recruiting people. He would tell them something like, "I can get you free rent for three months and $10,000 from the landlord if you'll join in a habitability lawsuit." He would go into these buildings where there were thirty or forty apartments and try to get twenty tenants together, and then they'd file a million-dollar lawsuit. Of course, he took his 40 percent cut plus costs.

The tenants he'd recruited would go into court, and he would coach them on what to say. Frankly, they would lie, for lack of a better term. One woman literally dumped her kid in sewage just so they could take a picture and say, "This is how we have to live." They'd find a dead rat in the crawlspace and they'd put it in a unit and take pictures.

We went to court, and I was shown all these horrible images. They grilled me, "Well, is this unit five? Does it look like this?" All I could say at the time was "I don't think so." I didn't know the condition of every apartment in my head. As a result of this hoax, we came up with our strategy of documenting everything.

The tenant attorney had used the exact same pictures in separate cases. In one, he claimed, "This is apartment thirty-two, and look at the mold here." But in a case involving another landlord, he used photographs he'd taken at a different building: "This is apartment seventy-six, and look at the mold here."

Someone on our side pointed out, "I've seen that picture before. I know I've seen that picture before." We tracked down the case. I filed a lawsuit. "Look," we said to the judge, "This is all fabricated." The lawyer had an all-purpose picture that he was using in various cases: the mold-in-the-apartment picture. He had been winning cases with it because the owners didn't have documentation to prove otherwise.

Still, I learned you can't really win when you sue an attorney. It costs you a fortune. I spent $75,000 suing him, and it cost him nothing. Basically, I got a $10,000 settlement. From an economic standpoint, it wasn't a good thing, but this tenant attorney who was the scourge of Oakland never bothered me again after that.

🏠 *Avoid going to court whenever possible.*

Avoid going to court whenever possible. It doesn't matter if you're wrong or right. The only people who make money are the lawyers. That's especially good advice in landlord-tenant law because usually the people whom you are evicting have relatively few assets. To them, you're the "deep pocket."

COSIGNERS, SECURITY DEPOSITS

To protect the landlord's interests, I'm a strong believer in cosigners. Obviously, a big deposit works well to get better compliance because people don't want to lose money. But the truth is that no matter how big your deposit is, it costs a whole lot more to fix up a trashed apartment. If you have a questionable tenant moving in, you are better off finding a responsible party to cosign the lease.

The cosigner is not going to want to write the check for unpaid rent or damages and will put pressure on the tenant to take care of matters. I can't tell you how many times we've had a young person move into an apartment and we had grandma cosign. A few months later, the tenant has been partying a little bit too much and somehow lost his job and can't pay the rent. A phone call to grandma does wonders. You don't necessarily have to take action against grandma. She is going to take action in her own way.

You just call and say, "Mrs. Smith, when Joe moved in seven months ago, you cosigned, and I want to just let you know what's happening. For the last two months, he hasn't paid the rent and we're really concerned. Frankly, if we can't get payment by next Wednesday, we're going to have to file an eviction, and ultimately, you're going to have to pay for it anyway. Can you have a talk with him and see what's going on?" All of a sudden, Joe comes in with two months of rent payment. Whether he got it from family, we don't know. All we know is things suddenly changed. You can be sure that grandma had something to say.

EARLY INTERVENTION

In dealing with tenants who aren't paying their rent, you should nip the problem in the bud. Be fair, but be firm. We have empathy for people when something happens or they are facing difficulties, but ultimately, your job is to help them find a way to come up with the rent, not be the bank of last resort. "My hours were cut back at work. I'm not going to be able to pay the rent on time this month." That should set off your alarm bells. Your internal response should be "Well, you're not making your car payment late. You're not paying Visa late. For some reason, you think you can pay me late." Be firm. They're looking for the path of least resistance.

If you have to serve them a notice, you can say, "Look, we're not the bank. We're not a zero interest lender of last resort. Here are some avenues you can take." You should have a list of suggestions prepared, including asking whether the tenant can do a cash advance on the credit card or whether family can help. Of course, if there is a cosigner, you could say, "Do you realize grandma's the cosigner, and if you don't pay, she's going to pay?" You can have a list of agency resources. "If you call 211, they have one-month, emergency, rent payment assistance if you qualify." Go down the whole list.

The goal is to help your tenants find a way to pay you. You don't want nonpayment to become their habit. I've learned that if tenants get more than a month behind on their rent, no matter how good their intentions, it's hard for them to catch up. If it gets beyond two months' rent, they rarely will catch up.

Your strategy should be to contact them frequently. Call them right away when they are late with the rent. If they say, "I can't pay now, but I'll be able to pay you on the fifteenth," ask whether they can borrow from someone to pay you right away. If that doesn't work, keep calling. Call on the tenth to say, "Just checking in; we're still set for the fifteenth, right?" Then send a letter or an e-mail, saying, "Per our discussion, we will be paid in full on the fifteenth."

Send a reminder two days before that date and on the day before as well. Then, if you don't get paid on the fifteenth, you need to act. You've built your case that you've done everything you can to work with them.

Keeping on top of the situation really helps. When tenants are sluggish with their checks, contacting them swiftly and frequently is the key to getting the money to come in. Most such cases can be cured if dealt with early, and you can offer a payment plan if the rent is late.

If you take over a troubled building where some people are not paying at all and others are paying late, you may find yourself not worried as much about the late payers because you have to deal first with the nonpayers. Or perhaps you need to spend your time filling vacancies, not cracking down on lateness. That's understandable but not acceptable. If you don't address tardy payments, you soon will find that those payments come in later and later. The tenants perceive that they can get away with it.

You might say, "Well, at least I do get the late fee every month. It's not so bad that they pay on the twenty-fifth for the month." That works for a while until there's a hiccup. If tenants have regularly and faithfully paid on time but one day lose their job or their hours are cut back, they might ask for more time to pay, and you will probably get a check by month's end. But if someone routinely pays late and you have been tolerating that, you're just setting yourself up for a serious problem if something goes wrong. Suddenly, the chronic lateness extends to a month or longer.

Some tenants who signed a contract agreeing to pay you on the first of the month may claim they can pay you only at midmonth because that's when they get their paycheck, even though you know they get a biweekly check on the twenty-fifth as well. If you feel so inclined, you could offer a temporary payment plan to get them back on track. Tell them, "We need you to get back to where you can pay your rent on the first again. If you are paying all your other bills on the twenty-fifth, instead of paying us, you need to switch that. Here's what we'll do. We'll sign a payment plan to give you three months or so to work out your finances. During that time, we will not charge you any late fees. Pay us a half-month's rent with each of your biweekly paychecks. Use the other half to pay your bills. Then adjust your budget so that you're paying us the total monthly due with the early check and using the later check for your other bills.

If you do make such an offer, it needs to stipulate that the tenants aren't claiming a problem with the property. The payment plan needs to make clear that the tenants are agreeing to the plan because of their own financial situation, which has nothing to do with problems in the building or habitability. That way the tenants aren't likely to prevail in court if they make such a claim against you.

It's a headache to chase people down for money. It's a headache to deal with collections. But your goal needs to be to get everyone who has fallen behind back on track, and any early intervention you can do will keep those headaches to a minimum.

YOUR BEST DEFENSES

It is essential that you have a good rental agreement. You may be able to get one from your apartment association, but usually they are not strong enough. Consult a variety of resources to find a good starting point for your rental agreement. Over time, as you experience issues with tenants, you will want to add clauses to address those issues and avoid future problems. Your best defense against problem tenants is to have a strong, clear rental agreement and house rules.

🏠 *Your best defense against problem tenants is to have a strong, clear rental agreement and house rules.*

You also need an adequate security deposit. Some landlords offer $99 security deposits, but those are risky and the landlords often get burned. The only time you could reasonably offer such a deposit is when the tenant has great credit and would not do anything to put a ding in it. You would basically be relying on the tenant's credit history, not the deposit, for your sense of security. For tenants with lesser credit scores, you obviously need a much larger security deposit. In lieu of a cosigner, a sizable security deposit is crucial for your protection against people who don't pay or who cause damage.

Another good defense is your move-in and move-out checklist, with specific conditions documented in detail. When doing your walk-through, remember that a picture is worth a thousand words. A photograph of the carpeting's condition upon move-in, for example, is much stronger than a notation with a rating of one, two, or three. Recently, I was at an apartment where a brand-new carpet had been installed a year before. The apartment smelled of dog urine. In the middle of the carpet was an indelible red stain. We tried cleaning it to no avail. We had to pull and replace the carpet. The tenant who had been there for the year had skipped, and I would not likely see any money from her. However, her father was the cosigner, and in such cases, you may be able to track a tenant down.

WRITTEN REPAIR REQUESTS

A smart defense is to establish a policy requiring a written request for repairs. This can help you in court. A lot of times, tenants will proclaim things such as "I've asked three times for them to fix this leaky toilet," or "I have no hot water in my kitchen sink," or "The water pressure is too low and they haven't done anything about it."

Tell your tenants that if it's important enough to tell you, it is important enough to tell you in writing. You can make it easy, but make it a system that you follow. Tell tenants they can call you but the call must be followed up with a written request, whether by filling out a work order form or simply sending an e-mail. If they don't do so and later make claims against you, your argument will be (1) you have a policy that all requests must be in writing, (2) you make that clear to all tenants when they call, and (3) if it wasn't important enough to write down, how horrible could it have been?

You have a strong case when you can establish that the complaining tenant did not follow the policy that all your other tenants follow. If there's no record of the request, then perhaps the tenant was just thinking about it but didn't tell anyone or mentioned it offhand to a maintenance worker who was doing something else at the time. That hardly fulfills your clear and consistent policy. That policy is for the good of the entire community; if someone notices a serious maintenance issue that needs immediate attention, you want to make sure that it comes to the attention of the management. A verbal request to the guy cutting the lawn can easily be forgotten, and that's why you must not allow that. Remind all your tenants of your policy regularly, at least once a year.

IS THE LANDLORD PART OF THE PROBLEM?

A landlord's own leniency in rent collection and on policies can contribute to the problem. When a tenant says, "I can't pay you until the fifteenth," some landlords reply, "You really need to pay, but okay." Then they don't do anything and the fifteenth comes and goes. On the sixteenth, they ask the tenant what's up, only to hear, "Oh, well, I'll have it in a week." They end up dragging out the problem.

Remember always that you are running a business. You want to run a friendly business, of course, but any business gets less friendly when the customers aren't paying. You are providing your tenants with housing. To do so, you have commitments: you have to pay the gardener, the water bill, and the maintenance staff. You have to take care of your mortgage. The tenants need to understand why you must be a stickler for collecting rent. If they are late, they face a penalty. If they simply do not pay, there will be serious consequences.

We recently had tenants whose son was killed. It was a horrible situation. That month, they didn't pay their rent. They were dealing with funeral costs and other things, and we didn't push them on it. But several months later, they were still a month behind on their payments. When it gets to that point, you will hear any number of excuses. You'll hear that the only reason the tenants are behind is because of the late fees, or you'll hear complaints that something wasn't done. When you violate your own rules and try to be nice, it can become a lose–lose situation. It happens. I know. Occasionally I don't follow my own rules, and then I regret it.

It's best not to stretch your grace period for payment, and you may be better off having no grace period at all. Always enforce your late fees, and when the payment finally does come in, apply it to any late fees before giving credit for the rent payment. That's a critical piece of policy that we note on the first page of our lease. We call it "allocation of money received." We spell out how we apply payments, no matter what the tenant notates on the check. First, the money goes to any repair expenses that the tenant is legally liable to pay, then to late fees and charges, then to overdue rent, and then to current rent. The key is to be clear about that policy and enforce it. Otherwise, those late fees tend to just float. The tenant would prefer to forget about them, but you see them coming up on your ledger.

RENT COLLECTION STRATEGIES

To keep the tenant clear about how much is owed for what, you should mail or e-mail, a few days before the rent is due, a statement that shows the balance as rent due. A week before the due date, you can send all your tenants statements showing the amount owed. Another strategy is to use statements only as a collection tool for delinquent tenants so that obligations such as late fees are harder for them to conveniently forget. They'll keep popping up as rent due.

You could require that tenants pay their rent via electronic funds transfer. We only require it at the move-in, but I would encourage it because it's easier. You put yourself at risk if you allow new tenants to just write you a personal check for their first month's rent and deposit, and then you give them the keys. If the check bounces, you'll have to try to collect. It's a deadbeat tenant's dream come true. You have someone who has taken occupancy and who has paid you zero, and now you may be wasting three months of time and money pursuing an eviction. The deadbeat proceeds to trash the unit until he finally moves on to find another landlord to victimize. People have been known to go from place to place doing that. You always want certified funds before letting a tenant gain occupancy.

From a convenience standpoint, if you can get people to allow you to draw the rent directly from their bank account monthly, so they don't have to think about it, you'll get your rent on time. If you take credit cards, which is pretty easy for landlords to do these days, that method is convenient for tenants. You have to figure out the cost and how you want to handle the transaction: a charge of 3 percent on a $1,000 rent is $30, which adds up over time. You might cover that expense by charging residents a convenience fee. Or you may find that it makes sense to absorb the cost because you can collect your rents a lot more quickly and easily.

Years ago, tenants started telling me that they didn't generally use checks. In fact, the only check they ever wrote, they said, was their monthly rent payment to me. That led me to realize it was time for a change. I have a number of tenants who pay me using the online bill-pay system on their bank account's website. The bank cuts a check, but from the tenants' point of view, it's just a debit from their account.

Anything that makes it easier to pay you is a good thing, whether electronic fund transfers or payment by credit card. You could operate so that tenants pay you as they would for a gym membership: people sign up and grant permission for the gym to charge their credit card every month. The easier it is, the less of an issue it is. If the tenants don't have to think about it and the money just disappears from their account, that's about as easy as you can get. If they get a statement that reminds them the rent is due, that's easier for them than having to remember it's due. If you've got a convenient way to get it so that they don't actually have to deliver it to you, that makes it easy. Easy is the key.

TAKING BACK CONTROL

Whether the issue you face from tenants is as typical as a late payment now and then or as extreme as drug dealing, you can be sure that things will get worse if you don't act. You need to establish that you are in control of your property.

Sometimes landlords tolerate problems and don't raise rents because they are aware of repair issues and potential code violations. They know that tenants are aware of those issues and could call the code enforcement office, and so they tread lightly. It's a policy based on fear, and it will lead to ever-worsening conditions. Don't get caught in that trap. If you are aware of code and repair issues, deal with them.

Then you can work more aggressively toward improving the quality of your tenants. First, screen new tenants carefully. Bad tenants almost always get in because the owner did not bother to screen their background. Verify their identities and birth dates. Check their credit and references. Do what you must to make sure you know whom you are dealing with.

When you do get tenants who become consistently troublesome and develop into a huge problem, you can offer to forgive their debt if they move out in a week. You can even provide a moving allowance. That can be cheaper than the alternatives.

If you need to take back control over a property, you must send the message that things have changed, that this will be the way you do business. Put your policies in writing, and conduct your affairs professionally. It's important to act because tolerating bad tenants will drive good ones away.

You may need to get started by collecting the rent from door to door. That certainly will signal a determination to change matters. Sometimes when we took over management of a property, we would drop a debris box on the property the first day. In advance, we'd send around a notice saying, "On Wednesday, we're taking over management of the property. This is what we're trying to achieve. Here are some other buildings that we run and what they look like. We're going to make your place a nice place to live. We're going to start with a cleanup day. We will place a debris box on the property, immediately, for free disposal of any junk you want to discard." That too signaled how serious we were.

You have to plan to send an immediate and strong message that you will be doing things differently. Those residents who have taken advantage of neglectful management will probably decide to move on to easier territory. By establishing yourself as clearly in control, you will be reclaiming your property, enhancing its value, and improving the lives of those who provide you with your livelihood. By consistently treating all tenants firmly and fairly, you will be demonstrating to your community that you care and, ultimately, that's what will define your success.

THE NEXT STEP

Creating Value Now

We have gone through a lot of ways to transform your rental property operation into one that markets to, appeals to, and attracts the best tenants to transform your income, financial security, and business life. In most businesses, it is easy to see that focusing on the customer experience gives businesses an edge. Just as in sports, you improve your score by improving your performance skills and your strategy. But for some reason, in rental property, too many owners and managers are more focused on the score than on *what gets them* the score.

Now armed with a collection of strategies and real-life examples to successfully transform your property, you can start imagining yourself working with residents who can't imagine ever leaving. You'll have a property where residents are willing to pay a premium to live there, a property where friends of the residents are contacting management, before there is even a vacancy, to rent the next apartment that becomes available.

It can be your reality if you are willing to work for it. Adding value to your rentals requires strategic planning and careful consideration of how you best can serve your tenants. You need to consider market and trends. To add value, you need to think about how to transform a property so that it becomes not only your dream but your tenants' dream as well. It is really not that hard. I've done it time and time again.

The key is to appeal to what the resident wants. A smart landlord strives to appeal to today's market and to people's emotions. If you are to succeed as a landlord, you must not just offer a good place to live but also present it in a way that will fulfill your tenants' expectations. You must understand how they define themselves.

Remember that everyone wants good value, but they also want more: they want the best they can get. That's why, for example, some people are willing to pay a higher price for a new Mercedes or BMW rather than just buy anything that can get them from point A to point B. People buy an image of how they wish to perceive themselves.

🏠 *People buy an image of how they wish to perceive themselves.*

If you create a property that people genuinely want to live in, you can dispense with the selling and focus on creating long-term customer relationships. You are competing for your customer's attention against other owners and managers. If what you provide stands out from the competition and gives renters what they want, you won't have the collection problems and other problems most landlords have. As someone once said, the difference between *helping* and *selling* is just two letters, but those two letters make all the difference.

You can absolutely succeed using the principles and techniques we've discussed. By embracing a new mind-set about the role of marketing and the relationship it creates with your customers and prospects, you will be able to use a rental property to increase your income. Appeal to your niche market's emotions, and create a property that commands higher rents while you own it, and make a profit when you sell it.

How do you produce the classic win–win that all landlords desire? You always keep in mind that emotional space. You pay attention to what tenants want and need. You do whatever rehabbing is necessary to meet modern demands, but you keep the psychology of the tenant at the forefront in all your planning and marketing.

There's an old saying: "Little hinges swing big doors." Small increases in income on a rental property can substantially increase the bottom line and the value. Let's say your rental unit brings in $10,000 a year. If expenses are $4,000 and loan payments are $5,000, that's a thousand dollars of cash flow before taxes. But if you could get your income up just 10 percent, to $11,000, with expenses and payments remaining the same, you would have $2,000 on the bottom line—twice as much profit.

		10% increase in income
Income	$10,000	$11,000
Less Expenses	– $4,000	– $4,000
Net Operating Income	$6,000	$7,000
Less Debt Service	– $5,000	– $5,000
Cash Flow	$1,000	$2,000

Becomes 100% increase in cash flow

Some of your enhancements may get you just 5 percent here or 10 percent there, though some could bring you much more. Even the small ones, however, will substantially increase your cash flow, and you can realize further gains through expense reductions, such as passing on some utility costs to the resident. That can go far toward increasing the property's value when you're getting a new loan or ultimately selling the property.

It may seem like common sense, but so few landlords are actually doing it right. By mastering these techniques over time, you'll turn renting out property into an art form and reap the benefits.

YOUR CONTRIBUTION TO YOUR COMMUNITY

Back in the days when I was fixing up houses, we would begin work on a long-neglected building and the neighbors would come by and tell us, "We're so glad you're here. Finally something is being done about that place. We've been waiting for this."

We had similar reactions from neighbors of the apartment buildings we later began taking over. Those buildings were certainly not the pride of the community. In fact, the best apartment building to buy, in many cases, is a shabby one because it presents so much opportunity for improvement—and profit. And neighbors follow your example. After we began work on the outside of such properties, it seemed as if the neighbors discovered the wonders of paint, and they would start beautifying their own properties.

Our positive example reversed a downward spiral and lifted the neighborhood. A landlord can reap not just great profits but a great sense of satisfaction for having improved a community. Remember that you are in this for more than yourself. What you do for a living as a landlord can contribute greatly to quality of life for your tenants and your neighborhood if your approach is one of compassion delivered with firm and fair policies.

It also takes time. You must visit the properties often, even when someone else is handling the day-to-day management. Recently, I handed a property over to a fee manager. It was 95 percent occupied and stable, and I felt confident in focusing on other properties that needed my attention. Soon, though, I was notified that the cash flow at the building had become a problem, and then the manager whom I had hired wanted to give up and hand the property back over. I was astounded by what I found. The place was dirty, and vacancy had risen to 35 percent. Next door, an apartment building with horrible tenants had gone into foreclosure. The neighborhood was slipping.

The first thing I did was hire a cleaning company to scrub the hallways, the floors, and the baseboards. We gave it a deep cleaning, its first in a long time. In the first month, I rented eight of the fifteen vacant apartments. It took about three months to get back up to 100 percent. This reaffirmed to me how the basics of showing that you care while providing an environment your tenants would want to live in can yield dramatic results, even if you don't have much money to spend.

By putting in the time and paying close attention to what is going on at each building, you will often sidestep instead of misstep. A broker recently told me that he advises clients interested in rental properties to look for the ones run by certain management companies that take the path of least resistance. "If such properties are in a good location and relatively free of problems," the broker said, "there's probably a good 10 or 15 percent of unrealized opportunity just because they're not tightly watching everything."

By being a good steward, marketing wisely, and selecting tenants carefully, you will get tenants who are delighted to stay and afford you a sense of pride. To do that, you must treat them well and provide them with comfortable, dependable accommodations tailored to their tastes. You must deliver the kind of service that you would expect for yourself.

CONTINUE THE CONVERSATION AT THEEFFECTIVELANDLORD.COM

This isn't the end of the story; it's just the beginning. The principles, themes, and trends noted in *The Effective Landlord* will continue to grow and expand. I'll be chronicling success stories and best practices and answering questions at the official website (TheEffectiveLandlord.com), where you'll find additional resources to help you on your journey toward reaching your goals. I invite you to visit right now and see what's available.

Remember, everyone reading this book has the ability to realize incredible success and achieve significantly increased income. But you're going to have to put forth some effort and incorporate a few concepts at a time. You'll experience a learning curve, but I guarantee it will be at a much quicker pace than the one I had to go through.

Work through the process as quickly as possible without rushing anything. Once you've mastered the techniques, you'll find great satisfaction and fulfillment (to say nothing of great results).

You can teach others what you have learned. Not only will this contribute to a great work environment but it will also teach you new things in the process. Revisit steps and sections as needed. You have all you need, so get out there, implement your new knowledge, and get ready for more success!

EFFECTIVE LANDLORD IN YOUR COMPANY

One of the biggest challenges I have faced after reading business books is the gap between what I've read and how to apply it to my own situation. If you're interested in thinking through how you can apply Effective Landlord processes and techniques in your own company or to your rental property portfolio, contact me. I conduct Effective Landlord audits and work with people like you to transform their properties and their businesses.

I sincerely hope you enjoyed this book. But most of all, I hope you found it useful and apply it—that's what it's all about. Share with me the successful ways you find to apply these strategies in your life. Please send me your results and breakthroughs. I collect and study all kinds of success stories, large and small. When I get yours, I'll send you a free report on a topic I think will be of interest.

To your success!
–Dan Lieberman

DAN LIEBERMAN

Milestone Properties
3640 Grand Avenue, Suite 206
Oakland, CA 94610

DLieberman@MilestoneCA.com

(510) 835-8080

For more resources, go to AskDanLieberman.com.

9 781599 324142